THE IS MANAGEMENT AND BUSINESS CHANGE GUIDES

HOW TO MANAGE SERVICE PROVISION

The IS Management and Business Change Guides

HOW TO MANAGE

Service

Provision

FORMAT
PUBLISHING

Published by
Format Publishing Limited
9-10 Redwell Street
Norwich
Norfolk NR2 4SN
United Kingdom

General enquiries/telephone orders: **01603 766544**
Fax orders: **01603 761491**
Email: **sales@formatpublishing.co.uk**
Online ordering: **www.formatpublishing.co.uk**

Edited, designed and typeset by **Format Information Design**

Published for the Office of Government Commerce
under licence from the Controller of Her Majesty's Stationery Office.

First published 2002
ISBN 1903091128

For further information about this and other OGC products, please contact:
OGC Service Desk
Rosebery Court
St Andrews Business Park
Norwich NR7 0HS

Telephone: 0845 000 4999
Email: info@ogc.gsi.gov.uk
Website: www.ogc.gov.uk

Printed in the United Kingdom for Format Publishing

Contents

Executive summary

Acquiring a new service can be time-consuming and difficult, but signing the service contract is just the beginning. Once a contract comes into force and a service comes on-stream, the emphasis shifts to managing the delivery of the service, the benefits that accrue from it, and the relationship between customer and provider. This requires a sustained effort and commitment over the whole life of the contract.

This guide discusses the major areas of service management: service delivery, the contract, the relationship, seeking improvements and managing changes. It also gives a brief overview of recompetition.

Services must be managed if they are to remain efficient, relevant, productive and trouble-free. Whatever the focus of the services, the fundamentals of service management remain the same. It is all about achieving understanding between customer and provider, delivering results, obtaining value for money and aiming to improve quality.

Good service management goes much further than ensuring that the agreed terms of the contract are being met. There will always be some tensions between the different perspectives of customer and provider. They must be resolved in order to build a relationship with the provider based on trust, communication, agreed objectives and mutual benefits.

Managing service delivery

In essence, managing service delivery is about ensuring that the provider delivers what is detailed in the contract, to the required level of quality.

When an organisation has awarded a contract for the delivery of a service, it must monitor whether the service is being delivered to specification. What is acceptable is normally defined in formal Service Level Agreements (SLAs), which set out the expected performance and quality of service. The content of SLAs must be reasonable and realistic, and some 'bedding down' – adjustments within the scope of the contract – may be required in the early stages of a relationship.

Measuring service quality means creating and using quality metrics – measurements that allow quality to be measured. These measurements will cover such aspects as completeness, availability, capacity, reliability, flexibility and usability. Some measurements will be binary (satisfactory/not satisfactory), some will be numerical or statistical, and others will be more subjective. It is vital that measures are carefully selected to give a balanced picture of all aspects of the service.

A key concept is value for money. As well as fulfilling the contract terms and delivering to the required level of quality, a service must represent value for money for the customer organisation throughout the life of the contract. Ensuring value for money means taking into account all the costs of the service, the benefits it delivers and the risks associated with it. It is not synonymous with lowest cost.

Benchmarking – making like-for-like comparisons between providers, often on price – can help to ensure value for money and also improve performance and business practices. Benchmarking providers helps prevent prices drifting out of line with industry norms over the life of a contract. It also helps to identify and prioritise areas for improvement.

Where service provision arrangements are complex, especially in cross-cutting initiatives, the important areas for consideration include who will manage risks in the whole supply chain (your organisation, your customers, your suppliers and their suppliers) and who will take responsibility for service delivery and any shortfalls.

Contract administration

Contract administration covers the formal aspects of the relationship, as defined in the contract. As well as maintaining the contract and its documentation, it also covers such areas as charges and cost monitoring, ordering, payment and budget procedures, resource management and planning, management reporting and asset management.

The importance of contract administration should not be underestimated. Clear procedures ensure that all parties to the contract understand who does what, when and how.

Managing the relationship

Building a good working relationship between customer and provider is vital. The people involved must be able to work together; they must know who is responsible for what and know what to do in the event of the day-to-day problems that will inevitably crop up. The relationship must be kept stable and workable.

A good working relationship is hard to quantify but no less important for that. It makes managing changes to requirements and handling recompetition much easier, when the time comes.

Good communications are always the make-or-break in managing a relationship. At the start of the contract, information flows should be established that define who talks to whom in each organisation, and at what level. Relationships should be kept peer-to-peer as much as possible, with clear procedures for escalating problems to the next level of communication if a solution cannot be found at the level where they arise.

It is vital to establish and retain intelligent customer capability – knowledge of both the customer's and the provider's businesses, the service being provided and the contract itself. There must be an effective interface between the customer organisation and the provider, managing the service demands of the business.

Seeking improvements

Managing service delivery, the contract and the relationship are essential components of service management. But they can only keep things running as they were at the start of the contract. There will almost certainly be a need for improvement over the life of the contract.

Public sector managers are under constant pressure to improve. In service management, this translates into a need for continuous improvement in the performance or value for money of providers' services. It is important that continuous improvement is seen as being desirable and beneficial for both parties, rather than as a means to drive down prices.

Improvements may be required by the contract terms, or there may be incentives in place (financial or otherwise) to encourage the provider to improve. For large-scale programmes of change, benefits-based payments are a useful way to link providers' performance to the realisation of the customer organisation's strategic aims.

It is important to avoid 'perverse incentives', that is, incentives that do not deliver benefits to the business. Providers should not be incentivised to improve one aspect of a service to the detriment of others; incentives must be realistic and balanced.

Managing changes

Change, whether planned or unplanned, is a fact of organisational life. Managing changes in service requirements is about making the process as painless as possible, and in particular ensuring that the contract continues to reflect current requirements accurately.

Change can happen for a number of reasons, originating on the customer's side, the provider's side, or from outside sources. Changes in demand, evolving business requirements, organisational restructuring (of either party), developments in technology and economic trends can all have an impact on contracts during their life.

Small changes may mean only a small amendment to service delivery or the contract terms. More significant changes may have more far-reaching consequences for the contract and the arrangement as a whole, depending primarily on whether they reduce or increase the scope of the arrangement. There may also be a need to change the way that the performance of the service is measured.

There should be a formal change control procedure, usually forming part of contract administration activity, which will help to manage the change process.

IT infrastructure management

Arrangements must be made for the management of IT infrastructure. Although this will almost certainly be carried out by service providers on the customer's behalf, it is important for the customer to understand the implications for its business. Design and planning are aspects in which the business plays a significant role. In addition, there must be processes in place for business continuity, to ensure that the business can continue to deliver its objectives in the event of things going wrong. There may also be a need for support for end-users in the form of training or service desk facilities.

Recompetition

Recompetition is what happens at the end of a contract – the exit strategy from the old contract and the process of creating a new one. The more strategically important the contract, the more attention needs to be paid to recompetition.

Recompetition should be considered even before a contract comes into force. A carefully planned exit strategy is an important part of successful service management, not least because it can help to reduce the potentially overwhelming competitive advantage of the incumbent provider at recompetition.

Properly handled, recompetition offers many benefits for the customer organisation, including the opportunity for better value, more innovative solutions and greater flexibility. It also provides an opportunity to re-examine the business need for the service, and reconsider sourcing options for the new arrangement. Once this is done, the scope of the new contract can be considered; this will involve looking at whether to retain the scope as it stands, broaden the scope, or split the contract into smaller components. If there are new or radically different requirements, the contract may need to be completely rethought.

There may be useful lessons to be learned from the experiences of other organisations, or opportunities for using an established framework agreement or another joint sourcing arrangement.

It may be that a framework agreement with more than one provider is more appropriate, or a wider-reaching agreement, perhaps a partnership arrangement, with a single provider.

Once a direction has been set, the handover from the incumbent to the new provider(s) must be carefully planned and managed, in order to ensure business continuity.

Introduction

Acquiring a new service can be time-consuming and difficult, but signing the contract is just the beginning. Once a contract comes into force and a service comes on-stream, the emphasis shifts to managing the delivery of the service and the relationship between customer and provider. This is no less important than acquisition, often more so. Consequently it requires a sustained effort and commitment over the whole life of the contract.

This publication discusses the major areas of service management: service delivery, the contract, the relationship, seeking improvements, managing changes and recompetition. It assumes that there is a sound business case for having the service, and that it has been acquired according to EC procurement rules where applicable.

Some knowledge of procurement has also been assumed. For a general overview of the procurement process, see the companion guide *How to manage Service Acquisition*.

1.1 What is management of service provision ?

Management of service provision is the process of ensuring that services provided by the private sector meet business need in terms of timeliness, quality and cost. Both parties to a contract must fulfil their obligations in order to ensure delivery of service requirements while achieving value for money. Managing service provision also includes managing the relationship between the parties and managing changes when the need arises.

There are many kinds of services, delivering many kinds of benefit. Services may be vital to delivering business objectives or they may support the organisation's main business activities. They may contribute to products or other services provided for customers, citizens, businesses, or other organisations. There may be one provider who provides a range of services, or many providers collaborating to provide a single service. Whatever the focus, the fundamentals remain the same. Service management is all about achieving understanding between customer and provider, delivering results, obtaining value for money and aiming to improve quality.

Managing services may involve complex interdependencies of providers and infrastructure, possibly involving several providers. Alternatively, there may be a single provider with whom the organisation hopes to build a productive, long-term arrangement. There will be relationships to manage and service quality to monitor, as well as the need to ensure ongoing value for money and service improvement.

Service providers may be internal or external to the customer organisation – in general, the same principles still apply, except that for internal provision the contractual arrangements will not have legal force, and both customer and provider will report to the same management.

This guide concerns what happens after the award of a service contract, not the procurement process that leads up to it. This guide assumes that the formal procurement process, as described in the companion guide *How to manage Service Acquisition*, has been followed correctly. This should have ensured that the acquired service fulfils a business need and will contribute to the organisation's strategic objectives, and that the contract is satisfactory to both parties.

1.2 Why is management of service provision important?

'The pressure never stops. Some people think that once you have signed the contract, that's it. In fact, you never stop negotiating. With large, wide ranging services there's always something that needs to be agreed or discussed or just plain argued about. Our relationships are good but that doesn't change the fact that you, as the customer, and the provider are approaching things from very different perspectives.'

Service manager in government department

Services must be actively managed if they are to remain efficient, relevant, productive and trouble-free. They must also continue to deliver the value for money that they represented at the time of acquisition.

With major services come major concerns. If customer organisation's requirements and the services that should meet them diverge, the consequences are significant: serious financial waste in the short term, and a catastrophic drift away from high-level strategic objectives in the long term.

The customer is responsible for ensuring that services support its business objectives and remain value for money over the whole life of the contract. The procurement process, if followed correctly, should ensure that this is the case at the outset of the arrangement. To ensure ongoing value for money, services and relationships must evolve. This ensures that the customer continues to get what has been agreed, and also that the provider is satisfied with the way things are going.

New ways of delivering outcomes place an even greater emphasis on good service management. The e-government strategy encourages innovation to deliver services electronically or over the internet. Service management is a vital component of such arrangements, since the situations are likely to be new to either or both of the parties, and the right approach can go a long way towards smoothing the delivery process.

1.3 New approaches, new attitudes

Good service management goes much further than ensuring that the agreed terms of the contract are being met – this is a vital step, but only the first of many. No matter what the scope of the contract, there will always be some tensions between the different perspectives of customer and provider. Managing services is about resolving or easing such tensions to build a relationship with the provider based on communication, mutually compatible objectives and benefits to both customer and provider.

Increasingly, public sector organisations are moving away from traditional, adversarial methods of service management and towards building constructive relationships with providers. A key concept is 'organisms, not machines'. While the terms under which a contract is to be fulfilled may be rigidly mathematical or assessed in a 'binary' way (the requirement has either been met or it hasn't), it does not follow that the relationship between customer and provider must be handled in a mechanistic way. Agreements, models and processes form a useful starting point for assessing whether the contract is performing well, but communication, trust, flexibility and diplomacy are the key means through which it can be kept in line. Adversarial approaches will only increase the distance between customer and provider.

1.4 Getting the contract right

This guide concerns customer activities following the award of a service contract, not the procurement process that leads up to the award of contract. But a key point is that the foundations for service management are laid in the stages before contract award, including the procurement process. The terms of the contract should set out an agreed level of service, pricing mechanisms, provider incentives, contract timetable, means to measure performance, communication routes, escalation procedures, change control procedures and all the other formal mechanisms that enable a contract to function. These formal contract aspects form the framework around which a good relationship can grow. If the contract was poorly constructed, it will be much more difficult to make the relationship a success.

The contract negotiation process must take account of the requirements for service and contract management. It is vital to build a contract that not only identifies clearly the obligations of the provider (and indeed the customer), but also enables a productive relationship built on good communication and mutual trust. While the contract must be built on a firm formal and legal foundation, it should not be so restrictive that it precludes flexible, constructive management of the relationship between customer and provider.

The companion guide *How to manage Service Acquisition* covers the issues around acquiring a new service contract, including the formal procurement process.

1.5 Managing IT services

It is a characteristic of today's business world that the role of IT has changed from enabling business processes to transforming the business itself. IT will almost inevitably be an important component of the services to be managed, especially where there is a requirement for electronic service delivery.

Today, the majority of private and public sector organisations depend critically on IT services to:

- deliver and present their products and services to customers
- support the delivery of operational services
- acquire and process the elements that make up many of their services
- manage relationships with customers, providers and partners
- control the flow of goods and services between customers, providers and partners
- manage internal processes
- monitor and control the overall performance of the organisation and its business units.

IT services may be delivered direct to the customer or – in the case of e-government – to the general public on behalf of the customer. Other organisations might also be customers of a service.

This guide will be particularly useful to those involved in managing IT services provided by an outside agency, although it will also be of interest to those involved in managing other kinds of service.

1.6 Who should read this guide

This guide is primarily intended for public sector managers who are involved in managing major services and their advisers, as well as 'intelligent customer' units or equivalents. Although the main focus is on services acquired from private sector providers, the guidance will also be useful to those whose services are delivered by an in-house team.

In addition, the guidance will be of use to the IT services industry in understanding their customers' expectations, concerns and priorities for the management of IT-related services, as this is the area where customers most often seek advice.

For more detailed guidance for IT service providers, consult the OGC IT Infrastructure Library (ITIL). See annex B for more information on ITIL.

1.7 Research for this guidance

This guidance has been developed from extensive research into current thinking and practice in the public sector. It builds on the work of special interest groups run by OGC with active participation from major public sector organisations.

The guidance also builds on earlier OGC best practice in service management and responds to lessons learned and the experiences of real-world practical issues, as reported by consultants in OGC's Consultancy Service and their clients. In addition, it incorporates feedback from contributors to OGC workshops and other review channels. These contributions are acknowledged with thanks.

Service management consists of a range of activities that are carried out together to keep the arrangement between customer and provider running smoothly. They can be broadly grouped into three areas:

- managing service delivery
- managing the relationship
- contract administration.

All three areas must be managed effectively if the arrangement is to be a success: that is, if the service is to be delivered as agreed, the formal governance properly handled, and the relationship between customer and provider maintained.

In addition, the arrangement must be flexible enough to accommodate change, and the process of changing must be prepared for and managed.

A key factor in all these areas is intelligent customer capability: the knowledge of both the customer's and the provider's business, the service being provided and the contract itself. It is vital that intelligent customer capability is established and retained within the customer organisation; it must understand the services that support its business.

2.1 The customer–provider interface

Figure 1 shows how service management functions with intelligent customer capability form the link between those who need and use the service and those who provide it – that is, between demand and supply.

Figure 1
The customer–provider interface

Service management and intelligent customer functions, in the centre of this diagram, form the link between business managers and users on the customer side and the provider organisation

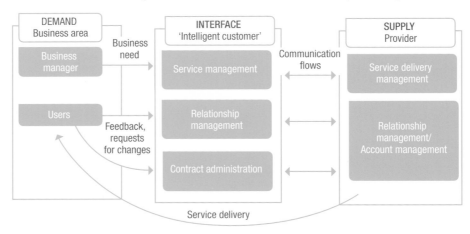

The business manager identifies and articulates the business needs that the service should meet. Users of the service provide feedback on how the service and the relationship are going, and may also request changes to the service.

In the centre of the diagram, bridging the gap between the customer's business and the service provider, service management activities keep the arrangement running smoothly.

These activities fall into three main areas.

- **Service delivery management** ensures that the service is being delivered as agreed, to the required level of performance and quality.

- **Relationship management** keeps the relationship between the two parties open and constructive, resolving tensions and identifying problems early on.

- **Contract administration** handles the formal governance of the contract and changes to the contract documentation.

Intelligent customer capability in all three areas provides an expert interface between the department and its providers.

Service management tasks will be carried out by a combination of roles: service manager, contract manager and relationship manager. However, depending on the size and complexity of the arrangement, it is possible that two or more roles may be filled by the same individual, or covered by the same team. There will also be a contract manager on the provider's side.

A key point is that communication flows must be carefully structured and controlled. Although the service is provided directly to users they should not raise issues directly with staff on the provider side, only with the contract manager or relationship manager within their own organisation. Otherwise, there is a risk that *ad hoc* requests for change put undue pressure on the relationship and ultimately affect the success of the arrangement.

Intelligent customer capability

Intelligent customer capability combines in-depth knowledge of the department and its business and understanding of what the provider can and cannot do. It is vital that the individuals or teams responsible for managing services on the customer side have this kind of capability. The aim is to reduce misunderstanding between customer and provider and to avoid mistakes before they happen.

Intelligent customer skills and experience must also be retained for the whole life of the contract, so that the organisation does not end up without enough understanding and knowledge of the services being provided to manage them effectively, or carry out an effective recompetition.

Intelligent customer capability enables the organisation to achieve the following goals:

- gain a common understanding between customer and service provider(s) of service expectations and possible achievement

- use service quality monitors as a basis for demonstrating ongoing value for money and service improvements

- manage ongoing change and the effect on relationships with partners and providers

- assure consistency in the use of IT and conformance with standards and procedures, making the user community aware of how to exploit the facilities to best effect

- preserve suitable flexibility in service arrangements, including in contracts, in order to proactively deal with unexpected changes and demands

- establish suitable baselines from which to track performance relating to service delivery and service improvement

- understand and influence the factors that preserve and enhance relationships to achieve maximum business benefit

- ensure that the benefits approach appraises the full investment in business change and not just the IT component

- ensure that business continuity plans are kept up-to-date to reflect changes and new service provision.

Experience shows that particular care must be taken to retain intelligent customer skills and capabilities in the IT arena – that is, the ability to set the direction and manage the exploitation of IT. With the lapse of time, there is a risk that key operational staff will have left, reducing the skills base beyond that necessary for the determination of technical requirements and evaluation of their delivery. This is, of course, a particular risk with long-term partnerships focused on added value services, where many staff will have transferred to the provider.

Managing multiple interfaces

For convenience, it is assumed in this guide that you have a single user or customer group and a single provider. In practice, you may have a wide range of customers with differing needs, both inside and outside the organisation. In addition, your contractual arrangements could involve a number of providers in a complex supply chain and/or a prime contractor with responsibility for the selection and performance of subcontractors.

Where service provision arrangements are complex, the important areas for consideration include:

- where risk lies (see section 3.4) and who will manage it

- the value chain: which services or service components add the most value, in that they make direct or critical contributions to realising objectives, perhaps in areas where the organisation lacks capability – the services that justify a greater amount of proactive management

- the supply chain: the dependencies between components of a service delivered by a number of possibly unrelated providers, and the risks associated with the underperformance of one or more components

- the end user perspective: the need to present a service that is seamless from the end user's perspective, no matter how many providers contribute to providing it

- different sets of customers: the need to tailor services to their specific needs.

2.2 Context

Figure 2 shows the context of service management: the contract management lifecycle.

Figure 2
The contract
management lifecycle

The contract management lifecycle runs from setting direction through acquiring and managing a service, round to recompetition and the start of a new cycle

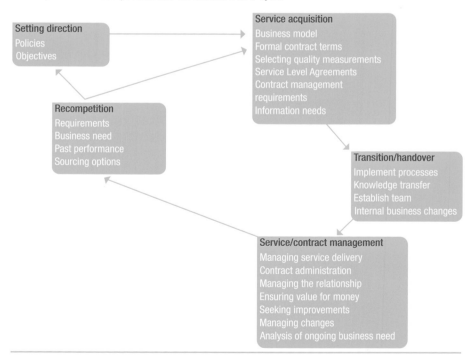

The lifecycle begins with setting direction: high-level objectives and policies for the organisation. This leads to the identification of business needs that can be fulfilled by acquiring a service. The service acquisition process is not covered in this guide, but is discussed in detail in the companion guide *How to manage Service Acquisition.*

Once the service is acquired, a period of transition leads into service management, which is the focus of this guide. A number of activities are carried out in parallel, the main areas of activity being managing service delivery, administration of the contract and managing the relationship.

When the contract ends, for whatever reason, the recompetition process includes a re-examination of business need, the performance of the existing service overall, any new requirements and the options for sourcing. Thinking from this stage may feed back into high-level direction setting as well as into the process of acquiring a new service: a process that mirrors the original acquisition but with the benefit of all the lessons learned from acquiring and managing the previous service.

2.3 Critical success factors

The following factors are essential for good service management:

- **Good preparation.** An accurate assessment of needs helps to create a clear output-based specification. Effective selection and evaluation procedures help find the right provider.

- **The right contract.** The contract is the foundation for the relationship. It should include aspects such as allocation of risk, the quality of service required, payment mechanisms, incentives, roles and responsibilities and so on, as well as procedures for communication and dispute resolution.

- **Shared focus on delivery.** Each side needs to understand the objectives and business of the other. The customer must have clear business objectives, coupled with a clear understanding of why the contract will contribute to them; the provider must also be able to achieve their objectives, including making a reasonable margin.

- **Service delivery management and contract administration.** Effective governance will ensure that the customer gets what is agreed, to the level of quality required. The contract's performance must be monitored to ensure that the customer continues to get value for money.

- **Continuous improvement.** Improvements in price, quality or service should be sought and, where possible, built into the contract terms. Determining a realistic baseline or benchmark against which progress can be measured is vital.

- **Relationship management.** Mutual trust and understanding, openness, and excellent communications are as important to the success of an arrangement as the fulfilment of the formal contract terms. Ideally, the relationship will improve continuously over time.

- **People, skills and continuity.** There must be people with the right interpersonal and management skills to manage these relationships on a peer-to-peer basis and at multiple levels in the organisation. Clear roles and responsibilities should be defined, and continuity of key staff should be ensured as far as possible. A contract manager (or contract management team) should be designated early on in the procurement process.

- **Knowledge.** Those involved in managing the contract must understand the business fully and know the contract documentation inside out. This is essential if they are to understand the implications of problems (or opportunities) over the life of the contract.

- **Flexibility.** Management of contracts usually requires some flexibility on both sides and a willingness to adapt the terms of the contract to reflect a rapidly changing world. Problems are bound to arise that could not be foreseen when the contract was awarded.

- **Change management.** Contracts should be capable of change (to terms, requirements and perhaps scope) and the relationship should be strong and flexible enough to facilitate it.

- **Proactivity.** Good service management is not reactive, but aims to anticipate and respond to business needs of the future.

Managing service delivery

3

This chapter deals with the practicalities of service management: ensuring that what has been agreed is delivered, to appropriate quality standards.

When an organisation has awarded a contract for the delivery of a service, whether from an in-house or an external provider, it must monitor whether the service is being delivered to specification. This means being able to check three things:

- the service does what it was required to do
- the service is being delivered well, to the agreed standards
- the costs of the service are no higher than expected.

At the most basic level, the service must fulfil the terms of the contract. If it does not, something is seriously wrong. It will not require any sophisticated measuring techniques to detect this. But the question of how well the service is being delivered is much finer. For example, it is easy to determine whether a telephone call is answered within a certain time, but much more difficult to measure whether the caller was happy with the result of the call.

Although numerical or statistical methods of analysis will be useful for many aspects, there will be others where standards are more subjective. It is the customer's responsibility to ensure that the quality of the service is satisfactory and that methods for determining this are up to the job. These measures may already be in place, or it may be necessary to create them.

Hand in hand with quality goes the question of cost. Improving quality may mean greater cost; reducing costs may mean compromising quality. Balancing the trade-off between cost and quality is what is meant by ensuring value for money.

The rest of this chapter looks at managing services to obtain value for money, as well as ways of measuring quality and the particular measures that are relevant to various categories of service.

The cost of measuring quality

Measuring service delivery should be planned and properly resourced, but it does take time and therefore costs money. Therefore it should always be kept to the essential minimum. To put this another way, while it may be felt that some aspect of a service is worth knowing about, or that assessing it would be of benefit to the business, it may be that measuring it is too expensive or time-consuming to be worthwhile. It is important to be realistic about the measurements that can feasibly be made, and to avoid letting unimportant measurements take up time better spent measuring core aspects of quality, or indeed on working towards improvements.

The provider's perspective

The provider is driven by the terms of the service contract and the payment/reward mechanisms it sets out. They may be free to vary the means by which the service is provided – for example, to reduce their costs, to reduce the risk of failing to meet targets or to improve the flexibility of their infrastructure.

They will almost certainly apply their own parameters to performance metrics, so as to leave a safety margin, and may implement internal controls to identify problems well before they compromise contractual performance levels.

The provider will expect to make an adequate return on their investment in providing services; their attitude to this will depend on the nature of the arrangement. If the contract focuses on economy, the provider may respond by running it 'lean and mean', with short-term profitability measures and a reluctance to undertake long-term investment. Alternatively, if the contract is within the framework of a long-term partnership, there may be a more open attitude to investment, evolution and to disclosure to the customer of internal issues and performance details.

Issues facing the provider include:

- meeting the customer's performance metrics with a sufficient safety margin
- meeting internal performance and profitability goals
- management of subcontracted services acquired to enable the customer service to be provided
- ensuring return on investment for capital and running costs in providing/developing the service
- optimising use of shared services/resources for the delivery of other services to the same or other customers
- risk management:
  - contingency/disaster recovery
  - change in customer requirements
  - level of innovation
  - investment appraisal/business case
- relationship management – creating and managing realistic expectations with the customer through effective two-way communication.

The end user perspective

As the old adage says, the customer is always right, even when wrong. The customer may be buying in services that are then passed on, possibly with value added, to its own customers. These end users are not interested in problems or excuses if service delivery falls below expectation; nor do they want service credits as compensation for poor service quality. All they want is the agreed service.

It is often difficult to embody this viewpoint formally in contracts. But examples from the private sector in particular demonstrate time and again that the most consistently successful organisations observe it closely and rediscover it frequently. All organisations can learn from this and it is vital to keep it in mind if service management is to be directed towards its proper goal.

3.1 Service level management

Service level management is the process of managing the performance provided to the customer as defined in the contractual performance metrics. Where the provider is in-house, a Service Level Agreement (see below) is used instead of a contract, as a legal contract is not possible between Crown bodies.

In order to meet customers' business needs and gain optimum customer satisfaction whilst meeting the provider's business goals, the provider has to optimise the relationship between cost and quality of the services delivered. Service level management plays an important role for the provider in balancing cost and quality of services in order to provide the customer with best value for money.

Well-structured service level management will help the provider to:

- quantify benefits and costs
- ensure that responsibilities are clearly defined and agreed
- charge for services delivered efficiently and fairly
- clearly define services and their deliverables (useful if services or service components are to be subcontracted)
- ensure that the services provided comply with the agreed business requirements
- have a better knowledge of current and future customer needs.

Service Level Agreements (SLAs)

Service Level Agreements (SLAs) set out a detailed agreement of the required service levels and thus the expected performance and quality of service to be delivered. They define the service levels and terms under which a service or a package of services is provided.

The Service Level Agreement states mutual and individual responsibilities. By clearly stating the required and agreed quality of services, both customer and provider know and understand the targets that have to be met in the delivery and support of services.

In general, the agreement should be a formal one in the sense that it is documented, signed and is valid for a defined period of time. The agreement should be concise, with a clear structure and layout. Each service level, with its associated terms and metrics, should be explicitly stated in the SLA.

The service provider is responsible for meeting the agreed service levels provided that the conditions stated in the SLA are met. If meeting these conditions is related to or affected by end user activity, then it is the customer's responsibility to ensure that these conditions are met.

Both customer and service provider are responsible for monitoring, revising and evaluating existing SLAs on behalf of their respective parties.

The period covered by an SLA is negotiated between both parties. When determining the timescales, the service policies and operational constraints of both customer and service provider are taken into account. Normally, SLAs are expected to be renewed annually but subject to six-monthly reviews.

Flexibility

Wherever there are formal agreements, on service levels as elsewhere, there is often a need for some flexibility. This is particularly true in the early stages of an agreement:

- mutual requirements must be reasonable – neither the customer's business nor the service provider will meet the highest standards overnight

- mutual requirements need to be realistic – in terms of technology, organisational capability and cost

- exception procedures must be catered for – neither customer nor service provider can be expected to meet the requirements under all circumstances

- there should be a mutual understanding of required service levels – both customer and provider must be aware of the other side's benefits, costs and risks associated with meeting or not meeting a service level. This is vitally important when finalising an SLA.

3.2 Measuring quality

Managing service delivery involves more than simply gauging whether services are being delivered to agreed levels or volumes, or within agreed timescales. The quality of the service being delivered must also be assessed.

Determining measures for quality

Measuring service quality means creating and using measures that allow the quality of a service to be measured. This involves the following steps:

- identifying the aspects of the service that need to be measured

- deciding how they are to be measured

- formalising the process.

Some aspects of service quality are:

- completeness

- fitness for purpose

- capacity

- availability

- reliability

- accuracy

- usability

- flexibility

- timeliness

- responsiveness

- security

- standards

- auditability

- satisfaction.

There may be others that are applicable; there may also be a need to modify, add or remove service quality measures during the lifetime of the service.

It may be too expensive or time-consuming to measure a given aspect; the time and resource implications must be borne in mind. If a measurement requires intelligent customer capability, a person or team who has that capability will need time to devote to the task.

Binary assessment   Some aspects of a service can be assessed in a binary way. They are the foundation aspects of a service; its most basic components. These aspects are either adequate or inadequate, with nothing to be gained by improving them beyond the level of adequacy. An example would be compliance with standards; if the service complies with the relevant standards, then it is satisfactory in that respect: no additional work need be done in that area.

Even though the quality of certain aspects is a binary consideration, some flexibility in how it is assessed may be desirable, particularly in the early stages of rollout. It may not be productive to point out a minor transgression on standards if the provider has worked hard to bring the service on-stream within a short timescale.

Strategic and non-strategic services

A useful distinction is that between strategic and non-strategic services. Put simply, this is the distinction between services that contribute directly to the organisation's high-level strategies (strategic), and those that facilitate or enable day-to-day business activities (non-strategic).

Non-strategic services can be evaluated in a binary way: they either fulfil the requirement or they do not. There is no point 'gold-plating' a service that only needs to be done well enough. For example, office automation systems rarely need to operate twenty-four hours a day, 365 days a year with 99.99% availability. Making them so would be costly and unnecessary, and deliver no significant benefit to the organisation. They need only work well enough to prevent them becoming a problem.

Strategic services are critical and need to be done as well as the organisation knows how. The better they are done, the more benefits will result. Examples of such services are the provision of business-to-consumer services via a web interface or call centre.

Numerical assessment

Some service aspects are measurable numerically; they can be counted and measured in a simple, mathematical way. Examples would be capacity, throughput, transaction volumes and accuracy. If the service is processing TV licence applications, the capacity metric might be expressed as the number of licences processed in a given week, and the accuracy metric as the number of those processed without mishap in a week. Such metrics give a snapshot of a service at a point in time.

It is relatively simple to create service metrics for numerical aspects; quality is expressed numerically, and there is a set numerical value, or proportion, that is deemed acceptable. Results that are greater than the set value represent an increase in quality beyond the required level. In such a situation, it would be important to ensure that the organisation was not paying for a higher level of quality than was actually required.

Although there may be some 'teething troubles' when new services are implemented, it would be expected for a service to attain stipulated levels of capacity and accuracy from its inception.

With continuously repeated measurements, simple numerical metrics give only repeated 'snapshots' of a service. To get a fuller picture of service aspects such as accuracy, reliability and timeliness, these measurements must be brought together to show changes over time. This means calculating averages, proportions, percentages or ratios – for example, the proportion of time that the service is operational, or the ratio of accurately handled enquiries to those where errors are made.

These values should also have acceptable levels below which they should not fall. Taking reliability as an example, it is normal to define an agreed level of 'downtime' for IT services. It might be deemed acceptable for a web site to be unavailable 1% of the time in a rolling twenty-four-hour period. For core business functions such as email and telecommunications, however, downtime might be deemed totally unacceptable between 7.30am and 7.30pm; 100% availability would be required.

During the acceptance period or piloting of a service, it is possible that reliability, accuracy and other such aspects may fluctuate. It is important to stipulate an appropriate period and duration over which to gauge quality. Too short a period might give an unfair picture; on the other hand, too long a period may be similarly misleading. A short period might make brief disruptions due to unforeseen factors seem overly significant, while a long period might smooth out interruptions or disruptions that were serious and should be examined.

The period to be sampled will probably be more informative as a fixed time than an ever-increasing period. For example, measuring accuracy from the time of the service's inception might be less helpful than a measurement of the accuracy of the service over the last six months. Such measurements also give a better idea of improvements to the service.

It may be desirable to stipulate a desired rate of change in a metric – for example, to process 100 licences a week for the first month and to seek a 2% increase on that figure in each following month. This would be a requirement for continuous improvement (see section 6.2).

For more detail on measuring quality through performance metrics, setting target levels and other issues, see the companion guide *How to manage Performance*.

The baseline

The baseline is the existing level at which the service is being delivered, either internally or through an existing arrangement. The baseline is normally established in the business case for the contract. Performance measures, and any improvements in performance, are tracked against the baseline.

It is important to set the baseline accurately in order to gauge how well the service performs, and how much value the new service is providing compared with previous arrangements. Where the requirement is complex, or where sourcing arrangements are not being renewed on a like-for-like basis, it may be more difficult to agree the level at which the baseline is to be set or even how it should be calculated. Since the provider's targets and performance will be calculated relative to the baseline, they will take a keen interest in this. Customer and provider must work together to set baselines at a level that accurately reflects the service the customer is currently getting and forms a fair basis for performance measurements.

Subjective assessment

Some aspects of a service will be hard to measure because they involve subjectivity: usability and flexibility, for example. However, it is still important to agree what is to be measured and how the information will be acquired – through user surveys, perhaps. Subjective aspects should not be neglected simply because mathematical techniques cannot be applied to them; it is a question of gathering information and analysing it with as much objectivity as possible.

It is unlikely that the usability of a service will be accurately gauged on day one of its operation. But over time formal or informal feedback on such aspects from staff or customers who use the service will be received. Involving staff at all stages of implementing a new service and documenting their reactions carefully are important steps in gauging its success.

Similarly, flexibility can only be gauged 'in the field'. While it is a given that services should be as flexible as possible, in terms of both their capacity and their scope, in practice it is impossible to predict all the demands that may be placed upon them.

It is the subjective aspects of a service that are gauged over the longest term, and where hindsight will offer the clearest perspectives. They are also likely to be the aspects that offer the most pertinent lessons to be taken forward to the acquisition of future services.

It is not always necessary or appropriate to use easily quantifiable aspects of a service as primary metrics. Where the service is delivered to a population of relatively naïve or casual users, it is often easiest to frame service performance targets in terms of what they find acceptable. This can usually be assessed by means of the levels of reported incidents or complaints. Even here, though, diagnosis of reported incidents or trends may well require deeper investigation, involving performance characteristics of the underlying infrastructure.

Legacy services

When a number of previously contracted services are being brought together into a single agreement, or where significant cultural and process change is being sought, it may not be appropriate to set new quality measures immediately. Existing legacy services may not be performing as contracted; performance may not even be being measured at all. Even where the service metrics are compliant with the existing contractual metrics, they may be unsatisfactory for some other reason.

In these circumstances, it may be best to start operation of the contract with a limited range of overarching, outcome-based metrics that offers especially strong leverage in business terms (an outcome/standard-based designation approach). There should also be provision in the contract for the joint evolution of a fuller, more focused set of metrics and associated diagnostic and remedial facilities and processes during the early stages of the contract.

In the case of legacy systems, it may be appropriate to assume that there will be a period of transition where:

- there will be no fundamental change to the performance metrics

- measurement systems will need to begin the capture of metrics that are not currently provided

- non-performing areas will be required to be brought within the existing contractual performance parameters

- improved performance will be sought where there is potential for it and business value can be derived from it

- performance history will need to be accumulated where it is required

- the relevance of current performance metrics will then be assessed, to see whether they need to be amended or replaced.

In the case of such legacy services taken over by a new service provider, the provider may want to base their performance on recent actual performance, as demonstrated by historic data, rather than on the contracted targets. There may be a shortage of such data in some cases, and thus no performance baseline whatever. It is as well to pre-empt this by assembling as much historic data demonstrating past performance as possible before the start of the contract.

3.3 Value for money

Quality measures and metrics provide information about how well a service is performing, from the basic level of whether it is fulfilling its function to more subtle considerations such as whether quality is improving over time and how satisfied customers are with it. But of course it is no good providing a perfect service if the costs are prohibitive. Ensuring value for money is all about the trade-off between service quality and cost. A key objective for the management of any service is to ensure that it continues to achieve value for money over time.

Value for money provides the common ground for very different services to be compared and their relative value to the organisation to be gauged; it is possible to ask of any service, 'is it good value for money?' and the implied (often unspoken) question, 'would the money be better spent elsewhere?' Assessing value for money creates a space for the consideration, in relation to a given service, of whether the same investment elsewhere would deliver better or greater value.

Effectiveness, efficiency and economy

Value for money comes from the effective, efficient and economic use of resources.

- **Effectiveness** is sometimes expressed as 'doing the right things'. It is a measure of the extent to which objectives have been achieved.

- **Efficiency** is sometimes expressed as 'doing things right'. It is a comparison of output with the input required to produce it.

- **Economy** is concerned with obtaining the same goods or services more cheaply.

The value/cost ratio

Getting value for money means optimising the ratio between value and cost. Depending on how precisely the quality of services can be quantified – that is, whether metrics are predominantly numerical or not – it may be possible to express the value/cost ratio very precisely. In other circumstances, the concept of value may be more subjective.

It is also important to track actual costs against planned costs, to ensure that the right level of resource has been assigned to a service.

Types of cost

The following types of cost need to be considered when assessing value for money:

- **one-time costs:** the costs of setting up a service in the first instance, including infrastructure investment, consultancy fees, and so on

- **unit costs**: costs incurred on a per-transaction basis, for example a fee charged every time a particular service is used

- **recurring costs:** costs incurred on a regular basis, for example a flat fee charged every month to cover provision of a service

- **internal costs:** the internal overhead of managing a service, including staff time cost, accommodation, facilities required and so on. These are sometimes referred to as 'organisational' or 'attributable' costs (that is, those portions of the organisation's overheads that can be 'attributed' to this service).

3.4 Risk

Risk is defined as uncertainty of outcome, whether positive opportunity or negative threat. In the area of contract management, the term 'management of risk' incorporates all the activities required to identify and control risks that may have an impact on a contract being fulfilled.

It is important to look at risks across the whole supply chain – that is, your own organisation, your customers, your suppliers and their suppliers – before making a decision on how best to allocate them.

Types of risk

Many risks involved in contract management relate to the provider being unable to deliver, or not delivering to the right level of quality. These could include:

- lack of capacity

- key staff on the provider side are deployed elsewhere, eroding the quality of the service provided

- the provider's business focus moves to other areas after contract award, reducing the added value for the customer in the arrangement

- provider's financial standing deteriorates after contract award, eventually endangering their ability to maintain agreed levels of service.

Other risks to the contract are beyond the provider's control. They include:

- demand for a service is much greater than expected and the provider cannot cope

- demand for a service is too low, meaning economies of scale are lost and operational costs are disproportionately high

- staff on the customer side with 'intelligent customer' skills are transferred or move on (possibly to the provider)

- the customer is obliged to make demands that cannot be met, perhaps in response to changes in legislation

- *force majeure*: factors beyond the provider's control disrupt delivery; for example, premises cannot be accessed because of a natural disaster

- fundamental changes in the customer's requirements, perhaps as a result of changes in policy, make the arrangement a higher or lower priority or change demand for the service.

Managing risks

Where risks are perceived or anticipated, customer and provider should work together to decide who is responsible for the risk, how it can be minimised and how it will be managed should it occur. The customer will be aiming for business continuity in all events, although it is unlikely to be cost-effective to plan for every possibility, and a certain level of unavoidable risk will have to be accepted.

Questions to consider for each individual risk include:

- who is best able to control the events that may lead to the risk occurring?

- who can control the risk if it occurs?

- is it preferable for the customer to be involved in the control of the risk?

- who should be responsible for a risk if it cannot be controlled?

- if the risk is transferred to the provider:

  - is the total cost to the customer likely to be reduced?

  - will the recipient be able to bear the full consequences if the risk occurs?

  - could it lead to different risks being transferred back to the customer?

  - would the transfer be legally secure (will the transfer be accepted under common law)?

Risk transfer

When a provider is made responsible for managing a risk, it is referred to as having been 'transferred' to the provider. It is important to remember that transferred risks still have to 'owned' by the customer, and cannot be forgotten about simply because the contract obliges the provider to deal with them. Providers will want payment for managing or taking on risks; ideally this will be built into the contract.

A key point is that business risk can never be transferred to the provider. Although the provider may be under severe penalties for non-fulfilment, this will not compensate a department for failing to fulfil its obligations and deliver key outcomes. For example, a critical service may fail, endangering the lives of citizens. Although the provider failed to deliver, the ultimate responsibility remains with the department. It is essential to consider the whole supply chain when analysing the risks to a contract.

While a relationship based on trust, openness and communication is desirable, a customer with too much 'hands-on' involvement in the provider's business can end up taking back transferred risk, by not allowing the provider to take responsibility for managing it. This take-back is itself a risk to the contract, closely linked with the issue of intelligent customer skills. A full understanding of what the provider can and cannot do should enable the customer to strike the right balance between 'hands-on' and 'hands-off' styles of contract management.

3.5 Benchmarking

Benchmarking is the practice of making like-for-like comparisons between providers with the aim of ensuring continuing value for money, getting better performance, and improving business practices. Benchmarking providers helps to offset the risk, in a long-term service arrangement, of underlying pricing and tariffs getting progressively out of line with market or industry norms. It also helps to identify and prioritise areas for improvement.

Some organisations encourage (or even require) prime-contractor providers to benchmark the companies they use as subcontractors.

Other benefits from benchmarking include:

- **economy** – lower prices and higher productivity from service providers

- **efficiency** – by comparing the costs of providing services, and the business contribution those services make, with what is achieved in other organisations. This helps identify areas for improvement

- **effectiveness** – looking at actual business objectives realised compared with what was planned, helping the organisation focus on strategic planning.

Comparing IT service provision, where exact like-for-like comparisons are rare, can be difficult. Process benchmarking – comparing processes used in the relationship with other equivalent organisations involved in similar relationships – can be useful in such situations. It is perhaps the most valuable of all the forms of benchmarking, if not necessarily in direct cost terms. Often a benchmarking club comprising like-minded organisations is formed for the purpose. Processes to look at include:

- demand management

- service planning and development

- service quality assessment

- investment decisions/project justification

- benefits management

- IT exploitation.

Many partnership arrangements, particularly those centred around delivering a business process, will be charged on a per transaction or per output basis. Benchmarking in such circumstances becomes even more problematic. It will be necessary to develop a peer group of organisations with equivalent outputs such as licence production or payment services. Benchmarking is unlikely to be usable for direct unit cost comparison because of the wide variety of potential business and operational differences, but it could be used to uncover general trends in unit cost movement and their underlying causes.

At a higher level, it may also be possible to benchmark the extent to which different arrangements are achieving their desired returns on investment, outcomes or impacts. The basis for benchmarking or the means for identifying areas to benchmark would be a tool such as the EFQM Excellence Model (see the companion guide *How to manage Performance*). Again this will be primarily about learning from other organisations' successes and, in conjunction with providers, translating those lessons into programmes of action or better ways of working.

Potential issues

There are numerous commercial benchmarking services that can compare, for example, costs per managed desktop, application development costs per function point and function point productivity.

The issues surrounding use of such benchmarks tend to revolve around:

- comparability of peer group in terms of scale, nature of business, infrastructure, risks borne etc

- recognition of costs/performance improvements made to date or that are capable of being made

- selection of cost quartiles such as lowest for price or higher to allow headroom for added value

- frequency of benchmarking exercises – the balance between keeping abreast of the market and overheads

- practical application of the results – for example, is there a negotiated or automatic impact on tariffs; is a performance improvement programme scoped and undertaken?

- to what extent special circumstances are recognised, such as the point in a technology refreshment cycle, the impact on the provider's business case or margin etc.

Because of the difficulty of employing competitive benchmarking in a fair and predictable manner, it is almost inevitable that these benchmarks become something of a safety net for protection against general excess charging.

3.6 Examples of measures

The following basic measurement criteria were adopted by a consortium providing IT services to a large financial institution. They are probably representative of many broadly scoped outsourcing deals. They illustrate the levels of performance measures, ranging from service level considerations up to business-level concerns and 'soft metrics' that concern the state of the relationship between the parties.

- **service levels:** the customer's business units have service levels by which they measure the consortium's performance. Detailed service levels include the following:

  - **critical metrics measure**: system availability, response/resolution time, on time delivery, on time/on budget delivery of applications, quality of applications, and compliance with certification requirements. Monthly and annual progress reports detail the performance levels

  - **operational metrics**: day-to-day performance of IT operations often serves as the foundation for critical metrics

- **customer satisfaction surveys:** surveys are conducted on a continuous basis, in various forms, to measure and track customer satisfaction

- **application delivery balanced scorecard:** specific metrics for applications development service levels are assigned, based on a variety of applications performance issues, including service quality, productivity levels, budget, future value, and client satisfaction. The consortium receives financial rewards if performance/productivity exceeds a specified threshold on a four-point measurement scale

- **high business impact problems:** actions are invoked for any disruption in service that in any way adversely affects the customer's business operations, processes or its own customers. Incidents are tracked over rolling periods of time

- **soft metrics:** the consortium members also measure their success by their ability to work toward the 'essence' of the alliance: keeping the principles of the partnership alive; creating an environment of trust, confidence and sharing; ensuring a consistency of thinking and approach to the relationship, and aligning all activities to the principles that the consortium is striving to engender.

There would need to be mechanisms linked to these measures, to reward good performance productivity and to discourage under-performance.

3.7 Business continuity

A major part of service management is considering what will happen if the service fails or is interrupted. It will normally be the provider's responsibility to manage service continuity, and this will be stipulated in the contract. However, the continuity of the business that depends on the service should be a jointly handled responsibility, agreed through liaison between customer and provider.

A key point is that the customer can never transfer business risk to the provider. Final responsibility for the business remains with the customer, no matter how long-term or involved the relationship with the provider.

Contingency plans

This is about maintaining critical services under a range of contingencies, ranging from minor breakdown of service components right through to disasters such as loss of a building.

Ideally, such planning is done top-down:

- it is determined which services are critical to the business

- a business contingency plan is drawn up that specifies how the business will continue its critical services under a range of disaster scenarios

- the consequent requirements for continuity for each critical service to the business are then derived

- service continuity plans may then be developed. Where services are provided by external providers, they may be responsible for such plans. The service contracts need to embody provision for such contingency arrangements. The tendency for providers to 'gold plate' such features – or to promise non-existent facilities which they believe will never be needed – needs to be watched for.

The above process may need to be iterative – the costs of a comprehensive contingency provision may prove prohibitive. The contingency plans need to be audited and tested from time to time. The costs of this may be significant.

Reviewing business continuity plans

In drawing up the contract, the customer should have considered the effect of a major breakdown in the service as part of the risk analysis activity undertaken in service planning. These plans for ensuring business continuity need to be tested periodically. The contract should set out provider responsibility in this area.

Reviews of business continuity plans should include:

- planning for action by the service provider to ensure continuity of service, where the provider is required to maintain the service. This is a service which the provider offers, planned in consultation with the users of the service and management

- planning by the customer to ensure continuity of service when the service provider cannot maintain the service, or when the organisation decides to terminate the contract; there may need to be provision for the service to be taken over at short notice by another provider.

See OGC's guidance on contingency planning and business continuity for more details on this topic.

Managing the relationship

4

A successful relationship must involve the delivery of services that meet requirements as defined by the contract. The commercial arrangement must be acceptable to both parties – offering value for money for the customer and adequate profit for the provider. But as well as these contractual and commercial aspects, the relationship between the parties – the way they regard each other and the way in which their relationship operates – is vital to making a success of the arrangement.

Managing the relationship comprises a discrete set of responsibilities and activities that, for larger contracts, may be assigned to a nominated individual – the relationship manager – or to a team. Even if the responsibility for managing the relationship is to be met by the same individual or team responsible for managing service delivery, it is important to ensure that the specific tasks of relationship management are carried out.

Section 10.4 lists the responsibilities of the relationship manager. The annex contains a list of questions that will help ascertain whether arrangements for managing the relationship are adequate.

4.1 Why relationship management is important

Service provision arrangements may commit the organisation to one provider or a small number of providers to a greater or lesser degree, and for some time. Inevitably this involves a degree of dependency. The costs involved in changing provider are likely to be high and, in any case, contractual realities may make it highly unattractive. It is in the organisation's own interests to make the relationship work. The three key factors for success are:

- mutual trust and understanding

- openness and excellent communications

- a joint approach to managing service delivery.

There must be mutual trust between customer and provider if the relationship is to work. The factors that help to establish the relationship and achieve the right benefits include:

- the provider gaining greater insight into the customer's business and management style, and therefore more often pre-empting changed requirements and/or making proactive suggestions/contributions, in the expectation that this may improve the service and/or provide other sources of mutual benefit; it may also incidentally bring them more business. In addition, the provider may also become more efficient and, therefore, cheaper for this type of service

- the provider feeling more confident in investing in the longer term – for example, in more flexible infrastructure, staff training and so on

- the customer gaining from knowing the provider's strengths and weaknesses, and focusing contract and service management effort into those areas where they will bring the most return.

Factors that can limit the scope of such a relationship include:

- the need to comply with EC and UK procurement legislation, especially where this requires regular recompetition in the open marketplace

- a clash of corporate cultures, where the business goals and planning horizons of the contracting parties are so different that there is little scope for mutual trust or regard – however, this may be safeguarded by suitable weighting in the evaluation process

- concerns that the incumbent provider may challenge attempts by the customer to test value for money, or compete on the open market for work that the provider feels falls within the scope of the relationship, or withdraw co-operation in other ways. Public sector organisations are typically shy of publicity, and are reluctant to tackle such challenges head-on

- difficulty in the formal procurement process in placing sufficient weight when assessing bids on intangible factors, such as 'do we feel that we can form a lasting, trusting relationship with this bidder?' It is often perceived to be difficult to justify accepting a higher priced bid because you believe it brings specific benefits

- the risk that the provider may not feel under pressure from potential competition and that their services may therefore deviate from best value

- concerns over confidentiality or conflict of interest if the provider has business ties with the customer's competitors

- risks to the provider that, if a high proportion of their turnover is dependent on one customer relationship, they may be vulnerable to pressure to squeeze margins

- risks to the customer that, if their business or services are critically dependent on a single provider, they may become vulnerable to price rises or to the departure of the provider from the marketplace for whatever reason

- concerns by the customer that too much business may overload the provider's management capability, resources or financial capitalisation

- in the commercial sector, the provider may even decide to set up in competition with the former customer.

Key factors for
management structures

Factors to be considered in establishing management structures for the relationship include:

- the need to ensure that the relationship is championed at senior levels in both organisations

- recognising that the attitudes and actions demonstrated by senior management will lead the tone of the relationship. The 'message' comes from the top

- ensuring that governance arrangements are equitable and relationships are peer-to-peer. If not, imbalances will occur

- a large number of formal management levels should be avoided, but some differentiation between contract management and relationship management levels is required to ensure a place for long-term strategic issues to be considered as well as the more day-to-day service delivery aspects. This separation is necessary to avoid urgent and pressing matters constantly swamping the longer view

- formal committee structures should not be seen as overly rigid

- roles and responsibilities should be clear and staff involved in managing the relationship need to be suitably empowered

- escalation routes should be understood and used properly – encourage an approach that seeks to resolve problems early and without escalating up the management chain unnecessarily.

An 'open' relationship – one in which people feel able to share problems, plans, concerns and so on – is often cited as a benefit or an aspiration for partnership approaches. Information sharing is the key to developing an open relationship.

4.2 Communication and culture

Good communications are always the make-or-break in managing a relationship. Many cases of mistrust or concern over poor performance in a service relationship result from a failure to communicate at senior management level, or from each party's failure to understand the business goals or intentions of the other.

Information flows

Many procurement projects are marked by an almost overriding concern not to expose 'our' (the customer's) thinking, position or concerns to providers for fear that providers will exploit such information for their own ends and to the detriment of 'our' interests. Encouraging the sharing of information can involve a significant change in practice; however, there should be a realistic balance of openness and reserving negotiating positions.

After contract award, the relationship can be developed by engendering a culture of information sharing:

- the objectives should be made explicit and discussed openly. This should have been a feature of the procurement phase but there is a need to keep objectives in view and revisit them from time to time

- sharing plans and information about potential future directions can help ensure the parties develop the relationship in line with changes in business need. This should be a two-way process. An understanding of where the provider sees their business going is as important as the customer's expectations if divergent positions are not to arise unexpectedly

- concerns about the relationship – whether about performance, progress or people – should be discussed frankly. If this is not done there is a risk that problems increase in seriousness instead of being addressed early.

Sharing information with providers may raise concerns about how information will be used. There may, for example, be a concern that information about the customer's plans, finances and resources will be exploited by a provider for its own commercial advantage. Willingness to share information openly depends largely on the element of trust.

These issues may be of particular concern where a multiple provider strategy has been adopted, but it depends on individual circumstances. Providers involved in the relationship may otherwise be competitors and sharing of ideas and information between them may be regarded as counter-cultural. If providers are in fact to remain in competition (for example, if the customer's strategy is to establish relationships with several providers and to allocate work over time through ongoing competition), it should not be expected that providers will be willing to share information with each other. If several providers are expected to operate in a collaborative manner, establishing principles and ground rules is important.

Information about how the provider views the customer should also be sought. Here again, a candid approach should be encouraged – although there is a need to avoid being defensive about criticism. The focus should be on providing and seeking information with a view to improving the relationship over time rather than apportioning blame.

Communication levels

In a large-scale service arrangement, the relationship between customer and provider operates at different organisational levels, with channels of communication running 'horizontally' between equivalent levels in each.

Figure 3
Communication levels

A partnership between a public sector organisation and a private sector company, with the three
levels of communication and the issues handled at each level

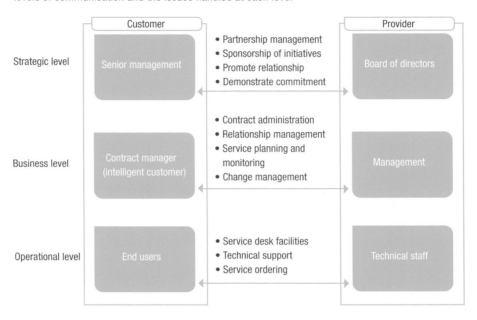

An example arrangement with three formal levels of communication is shown in
figure 3. Here a partnership arrangement has been created with a provider of IT
services, enabling the customer's long-term business strategy to be moved
forward. This large-scale arrangement has information flowing at several levels.

At the strategic level, the customer's senior management and the board of directors
of the provider company discuss the partnership, its management, and any initiatives
within it that they could promote or initiate. They also promote the relationship, not
least by demonstrating commitment to it and 'leading from the front'.

At the business level, the contract is formally managed. Services are planned and
their delivery is monitored. Changes to the contract are managed at this level and
most issues that arise will be dealt with here.

At the operational level, the service is delivered. Staff in the customer organisation
order or call off components as they require them and receive technical support
as required. The provider provides the service to agreed levels. Day-to-day
problems in the delivery of services may be resolved here; if this is not possible,
they can be escalated to the contract manager.

An important point is that the arrangement should be managed in such a way that
these levels of communication are preserved even when problems arise. In terms

of this diagram, diagonal lines of communication should be avoided. For example, if an end user feels the service is not being delivered to the required standards, they should refer this to the contract manager, who will liaise with the provider's management. It would not be appropriate for them to go 'straight to the top' and liaise directly with the provider's management; doing so will undermine the customer's contract manager. Similarly, it would be inappropriate for technical staff on the provider side to complain about their workload to the contract manager in the customer organisation.

So a combination of 'vertical' communication between levels within each organisation and 'horizontal', peer-to-peer communication between organisations is the ideal. It is part of good service provision management to ensure also that these arrangements are the best, as well as the prescribed, option for those with problems, and that no one feels that going 'straight to the top' is the only practical way to resolve them.

Another type of communication is that provided by the service provider's service or account manager function, which may operate at all levels. This has strengths and weaknesses: while it can provide a good channel of communication between the provider and users of the service, it can also allow users to request (or expect) changes to be made based on their feedback. These changes, if implemented, may not be in line with the strategic direction that the service should be moving in. They may also have technical implications, for example if a user prefers to use a favoured software application that is incompatible with other systems in place.

Consistency in communications

Consistent communication through the levels is important, or differences in perspective may mask problems in the relationship. For example, even where senior management regards the relationship as successful, serious disagreements and disputes may arise, and the relationship deteriorate, at the middle management level.

While there may be agreement at the strategic level about direction and overall progress, people involved on a day-to-day level may be concerned more with short-term aspects that may have a very different tenor to the strategic view. At this level people may have direct responsibility for monitoring service performance and authorising payment, for service delivery and revenue generation, and be managed as cost or profit centres. As workgroups and individuals, their objectives will tend to be set at the level of relatively short-term financial and delivery performance.

Behaviour and attitude   The way people involved in the relationship act and the attitudes they hold about other organisations in the relationship, and about the concept as a whole, are key determinants of success in practice. Trust is often seen as a defining characteristic of the relationship between customer and provider. Trust in this context may mean having confidence in the other party in relation to any or all of the following:

- capability to 'do the job' well

- goodwill – that the partner has the interests of 'us' and the relationship at heart as well as its own

- integrity – that the partner will act and speak in a way that is honest

- commitment to the relationship – beyond the letter of the contract.

While contractual and commercial arrangements may lay the basis for a relationship that is built on common objectives and shared rewards, trust is a feature of the relationship between people. Trust cannot be legislated for within the contract and although it may be anticipated (the customer may expect or intend to operate on a basis of trust), ultimately it has to be built and 'earned' through actions and behaviours, rather than assertions, and is tested when problems and disagreements arise.

Trust can seem a very intangible concept, but tangible efforts can be made to try to engender or promote a spirit of trust within the relationship. The principle and expectation that trust should be a feature of working relationships may be stated publicly and made a feature of internal awareness campaigns. Commitment of senior managers to the relationship must be visible and communicated throughout the organisation and reiterated throughout its duration.

In general, it is helpful to develop attitudes and behaviours that:

- respect the contribution of others

- do not emphasise the power of formal authority

- take a long-term view, with attention to longer term as well as short-term benefits

- look for benefits for all parties – aim for win/win relationships

- recognise the interdependence in the partnership and that the customer may directly influence the provider's ability to meet its objectives.

Everyone involved in the relationship should be ready to learn from the mistakes and experience of others. The emphasis in providing and accepting feedback on performance should be on using such information as a basis for improvement rather than penalty.

Those managing the relationship will clearly have a major influence on the way it develops and is perceived by people in the other organisation. Careful thought should be given to identifying the skills and attitudes of staff who will fill key posts and to the behaviours and personal attributes that are required and will be encouraged. This is not to say that customer teams should become a 'soft touch'. Commitment to managing the relationship and to long-term success requires active and assertive, not passive and submissive, behaviour.

Assessing the relationship   As well as measuring performance against financial and service performance measures, a means of assessing aspects of the working relationship and management processes should be put in place. This will be valuable in highlighting aspects that are perceived to be working well and those that require attention. For example, periodic assessments might address aspects including:

- the extent to which the provider is involved, or invited to become involved, in internal planning or other activities

- how well the management structures are seen to be operating

- how successful communications are seen to be

- the degree to which information is shared freely and openly between the parties

- whether feedback channels are seen to be working up and down organisational hierarchies

- whether conflicts are being avoided or resolved effectively

- whether financial and performance measurement systems are accessible to both parties

- the extent to which adequate monitoring information is being provided, and its quality

- user satisfaction and perceptions of the relationship.

Most such assessment factors are largely subjective but it is perceptions of how each party sees the relationship that matter. As with any change programme, it is helpful to monitor changes over time and to reflect back on progress in a way that helps people see the development that has taken place. A willingness to learn from mistakes, to be open about causes of conflict or poor performance and to be prepared to agree counter measures can all help towards improving the relationship over time.

The spirit of co-operation and partnership should characterise the relationship throughout. However, this must be tempered with commercial realism. Both parties need to retain a healthy sense of their own and their partner's objectives and strategies. If done openly in co-operation it will help to build mutual trust.

Depending on the arrangement, it may be appropriate to aim for continuous improvement in the relationship (see section 6.2). Improvements in communication, knowledge sharing0 and relationship responsiveness would all point towards such improvement.

4.3 Handling problems

However good the relationship between customer and provider, and however stable the services being delivered, problems will arise. So procedures for handling these should be agreed; clear reporting and escalation procedures help keep the heat out of the relationship. The objective is to establish a problem-solving relationship, in which customer and provider co-operate to ensure that problems are recognised and then resolved quickly and effectively.

The relationship manager should ensure that the provider has problem management procedures in place, including escalation procedures within the provider's organisation, and that these are used when needed. These procedures should seek to prevent problems as well as to resolve them.

The contract must define the procedures for undertaking corrective action if, for example, target performance levels are not being achieved. The customer response to non-performance should be commensurate with the severity of the failure. For certain types of service failure, the contract or SLA may specify the application of 'service credits'; procedures are required to calculate these and to enforce them.

Apart from service performance issues, problems can arise in a number of areas and for a wide range of reasons: clashes of personality; slow or incorrect submission of invoices; slow payment of invoices; problems with contract administration procedures.

Whatever the nature of the problem, it is vital that:

- problems are recorded as they occur, in order to highlight any trends and to help in assessing overall performance and value for money
- the provider is notified of problems by an appropriate route and at an appropriate level
- approaches to resolving problems are clear and documented
- escalation procedures are followed.

Escalation procedures

If a dispute cannot be resolved at the level where it arises, it will be necessary to involve a higher level of authority. This escalation process needs to be managed.

Escalation procedures should allow for successive levels of response depending on the nature of the problem and the outcome of action taken at lower levels. The levels for escalation should match those of the interfaces established between provider and customer. Every effort should be made to resolve the problem at the lowest practicable level.

For more serious problems, the contract should specify the circumstances under which the organisation would have the right to terminate the contract. The contract manager must consult senior management and purchasing/contractual advisors as soon as this possibility arises.

The contract manager should collate information on the number and severity of problems, as well as the way they were resolved, during the life of the contract. This information can provide useful input to IT service reviews.

The contract manager should periodically arrange for a check on the financial viability of the service provider, as well as continually monitoring any changes in ownership of the provider. Where potential problems are identified the contract manager should seek specialist advice as soon as possible.

Normally, most problems should be resolved before they become major issues; contract managers and service managers on both sides should meet regularly to discuss any issues promptly as they arise. In extreme cases, where agreement cannot be reached, the customer and provider should seek the assistance of mediators before resorting to legal action.

Contract administration

5

Contract administration is concerned with the mechanics of the relationship between the customer and the provider, the implementation of procedures defining the interface between them, and the smooth operation of routine administrative and clerical functions.

The importance of contract administration to the success of the contract, and to the relationship between customer and provider, should not be underestimated. Clear administrative procedures ensure that all parties to the contract understand who does what, when and how.

5.1 Elements of contract administration

The procedures that combine to make up contract administration are as follows:

- contract maintenance and change control
- charges and cost monitoring
- ordering procedures
- payment procedures
- budget procedures
- resource management and planning
- management reporting
- asset management.

These procedures will need to be designed to reflect the specific circumstances of the contract and the organisation. Bear in mind that additional administrative procedures may also be needed.

5.2 Contract maintenance

Contractual relationships evolve and must respond to changes in the business environment. It follows that the contract document itself must be capable of evolving efficiently and effectively, through formal change control procedures and by mutual consent, in response to changing requirements. It is preferable to update documentation as changes occur rather than relying on informal arrangements. Even in good relationships, disputes over detail (project deadlines and so on) do occur.

Keeping the contract documentation up-to-date is an important activity, but it should not be a burden. The effort required may be reduced by ensuring that the contract is sufficiently flexible to enable working level agreement and charges without changing the contract documentation.

Procedures should be established to keep the contract documentation up-to-date and to ensure that all documents relating to the contract are consistent, and that all parties have a common view. For a large or complex contract, or a situation where a number of SLAs are covered by a contract, a formal document management procedure may be required.

Applying document management principles involves:

- identifying all relevant documentation (including contract clauses and schedules, SLAs, procedures manuals etc)

- change control procedures, and ensuring no changes are made without appropriate authorisation

- recording the status of documents (current/historic, draft/final)

- ensuring consistency across documents.

New service descriptions and/or SLAs will have to be produced for any services that are introduced during the life of the contract – the introduction of new applications software into operational use, for example. If there is a change in the customer's organisational structure which affects the boundaries of existing services – for example the creation of a new business unit that is still supported by the departmental contract – the contract must be reviewed and revised as necessary.

The contract manager acts as the interface between the service provider and the rest of the organisation in handling requests for incorporating new requirements into the service contract. A preliminary investigation into the new requirement, possibly with the assistance of the service provider, will usually be required to determine whether it should go forward in the formal change control procedure (see section 5.3).

It is particularly important that additional demands on the service provider should be carefully controlled. In many cases orders for products or services may only be submitted through the contract manager. In other cases, especially where budgets are devolved, business managers may have authority to submit orders within specified budgetary and technical constraints.

Formal authorisation procedures will be required to ensure that only those new requirements that can be justified in business terms are added to the service contract.

5.3 Change control

Changes to services, procedures or contracts may have an effect on service delivery, on performance, on costs and on whether the contract represents value for money. So the specification and management of change control is an important area of contract administration. Change control procedures should be included in the contract. The respective roles and responsibilities of both parties in the change control process must be clearly identified, along with the procedures for raising, evaluating, costing and approving change requests.

A single change control procedure should apply to all changes, although there may be certain delegated or shortened procedures available in defined circumstances. A change control procedure should provide a clear set of steps and clearly allocated responsibilities covering:

- requests for changes
- assessment of impact
- prioritisation and authorisation
- agreement with provider
- control of implementation
- documentation of change assessments and orders.

Responsibility for authorising different types of change will often rest with different people, and documented internal procedures will need to reflect this. In particular, changes to the overall contract, such as changes to prices outside the scope of agreed price variation mechanisms, must have senior management approval. In many cases it will be possible to delegate limited powers to authorise minor changes which affect particular services or SLAs using agreed processes.

There should be an agreed procedure for placing additional demands on the service provider; these will include the specification of the requirement, the contractual implications, the charges for the additional service and the delivery timescales. This procedure should be used in consultation with those responsible for monitoring the service.

Appropriate structures need to be established, with representatives of both customer and provider management, for reviewing and authorising change requests. These may fit in with existing management committees, or may require new change advisory roles.

5.4 Charges and cost monitoring

The contract should specify the basis on which charges will be calculated for the services provided. Different approaches are likely for differing services. Operational services, for example, will usually be charged on some form of tariff basis reflecting the resources being used. Project and planning services will usually be charged on an effort basis, in terms of the number of man-days used, or as a fixed price. In some cases this may be a complex exercise – for example, ensuring that the charges for software maintenance are a fair reflection of the work done.

Examples of different types of service charges include:

- charges based on unit costs, such as charges based on usage of mainframe processing or data storage capacity

- 'baseline' costs for core services, charged at a flat rate irrespective of how much they are used (a service desk, for example) or charged in bands (£x for up to N users; £y for up to N+n users)

- fixed price quotations for work packages

- tariff arrangements with a disclosed target profit margin for the provider, and benefit sharing mechanisms.

In many cases the customer will have no material interest in the costs incurred by the service provider and will simply pay service charges as agreed. In other cases, contracts may operate with varying degrees of openness of provider costs. Such 'open book' approaches provide the customer with access to information about the costs incurred by the provider in delivering the service, and in some cases, such as where benefits sharing is a feature of the contact, to the provider's margin of profit. The degree of openness and the level of resource to be expended should be appropriate to the chosen basis of charging and defined in the contract.

Monitoring of charges and costs will help the customer to determine if value for money is being achieved across all services. It will also feed into discussions with the service provider on possible changes to the service provision or to the charges payable under the contract. Where service items are provided on a 'catalogue' or unit-cost basis, the customer will need to collect information on the pricing of such items with a view to renegotiating them as allowed for under the contract.

If the contract allows some level of price variation relative to an agreed index (such as the Retail Price Index), part of contract administration will be to ensure that variations in the prices charged for services are within contractually agreed limits.

Similarly, some contracts commit the provider to a specified reduction in unit costs over a set period, the achievement of which must also be monitored.

The customer-side contract manager will also need to monitor the overall cost of the contract to ensure that budgets for the service will not be exceeded. Internal costs, including the costs of contract administration, should also be monitored to ensure that these costs are reasonable and in keeping with the value of the contract.

Planning ahead to reduce resource costs

The most competitive charges for services or a specific type of resource may depend on providing a specified period of notice of the requirement. For example, software development staff may be charged at day-rates that vary depending on whether they are required immediately or can be planned for over three, six or twelve months.

The principle behind this is that the provider will be able to achieve better utilisation of its resources with longer planning horizons, and the benefits of the resulting reduced costs are passed on or shared with the customer through lower rates. One of the functions of contract administration is to ensure that business planning activities feed into the contract and service planning process in order to minimise the need for *ad hoc*, and therefore relatively costly, resources. The development of any revised internal processes for dealing with the new arrangement must take place in good time to be available for the start of the contract.

Where internal resources are made available to the service provider, such as site services, accommodation or equipment, the contract manager will be responsible for liaising with the provider on their administration, upkeep and maintenance and for implementing any cross-charging arrangements.

5.5 Ordering procedures

It is likely that the contract will specify a 'core' set of services that will be delivered on a continuing basis. In addition, the customer may wish to place new requirements on the service provider from time to time, according to procedures set out in the contract. Where the additional requirement has contractual implications, it must be raised through the change control procedure.

Whenever possible, the contract manager should plan for these additional requirements over the life of the contract. Orders for new services may be in one of the following categories:

- planning services, for example a requirement for consultancy support

- project services, for example a requirement for the development of a new system

- operational services, for example an additional requirement for an existing service provided to another part of the organisation.

Clear guidance must be provided and suitable processes instituted covering:

- who in the customer organisation may request and authorise services

- whether, and when, technical assurance or review of service orders is required, and who is responsible

- responsibilities for financial approval – it is vital to ensure that funds are available before ordering work

- who in the provider organisation may accept service orders and allocate suitable resources to deliver them.

In all cases the details of service orders should be recorded centrally to ensure co-ordination and accountability. In this way any discrepancies between services and service orders can be identified and checked, and any opportunities to reduce costs through economies of scale can be maximised.

5.6 Payment procedures

The customer and the service provider should have included in the contract the procedures for payment under the contract. These will include:

- structure and itemisation of invoices

- submission of invoices

- invoice approval procedures

- payment terms

- payment procedures.

Where charges are dependent on volumes/usage, it is likely that information for the calculation of such charges is supplied by the service provider. The customer must retain the right to audit such information.

Organisations will usually have existing procedures for paying invoices. There may be a need to ensure adequate co-ordination and liaison between, for example, business managers in receipt of services, the contract manager, budget holders and internal finance/accounting functions to ensure that invoices are correctly authorised for payment.

If invoices are submitted centrally or if budgets are centralised there may be a requirement for internal recharging or allocation of costs. This may be based on services received and workload or allocated on some other basis. To facilitate this, the contract manager should ensure that charging information from the provider is available at an appropriate level of detail and is in a suitable format. When a provider submits an invoice the contract manager must also ensure that the charges have been levied in accordance with agreed charging mechanisms.

Service credits

Service credits are a means by which the customer can be automatically compensated for poor performance by the provider. Service credits should be clearly linked to specific services and agreed service levels. Procedures for calculating and for making the credits should have been agreed during contract negotiation. The contract manager is responsible for monitoring the correct calculation and payment of service credits.

The provision of service credits from an internal provider raises particular issues. In the case of an in-house provider the cost of any additional service credits will be funded by the parent organisation.

A service that misses its quality targets by more than a specified margin in effect delivers no value, and any charge at all for it may be hard to justify. Remedies and service credits based on impact on the customer cannot always be made to reflect the margin by which the target is missed. For example, once a train is so late that the next one is due, the value to the customer of the earlier train has fallen to zero and it may as well not have run.

Service credits are generally a very blunt instrument in performance and quality management. Most people want a trouble-free service that runs to the standards set, not a poor service and service credits.

If a service credit system is used, it must be simple to understand and administer, to place the smallest possible additional demand on contract administration resources.

5.7	Management reporting

Requirements for service performance reports and management information should have been defined before and during contract negotiations, and confirmed during the transition period of the contract coming on-stream. It is likely that information requirements will change during the lifetime of the contract, which should be flexible enough to allow for this. Where possible, use should be made of the provider's own management information and performance measurement systems.

Information may be required about all performance measures or only about exceptions – that is, instances when performance differs from what was expected. 'Exception reporting' minimises the time the customer needs to assess performance and ensures attention is focused on areas that need it most. For many business managers a summary of the service they have received along with a note of exceptions is normally sufficient. However, the ability to access more detailed performance figures should be retained to facilitate trend analysis and investigation of exceptions.

Information from the provider about service performance may be sent to each business unit or to a central point – probably the contract manager – for distribution. The contract manager may be required to provide additional quarterly or annual reports on the service to customers.

During the early stages of the contract the contract manager should ensure that all information flows between the provider and the customer organisation, and between various internal groups, are identified and tested.

5.8 Asset management

If ownership of assets used in the delivery of services – such as hardware, software, office equipment, premises – is retained by the customer, then the customer will have responsibility for those assets.

In many cases day-to-day management of assets will be carried out by the provider, but the contract manager should ensure that:

- the organisation's asset register is kept up-to-date

- any third party use of assets is recorded (for example, if the provider is able to deliver services to other customers)

- upgrades and replacements are planned and budgeted for.

The contract manager should ensure that the customer is provided with an audit trail of technical changes made to the systems.

In some cases the cost of a service will depend on the equipment being used. For example, PC support services may be charged as a cost per PC. In such cases it is essential that the asset inventory is kept up-to-date as charges will be made on the basis of the information it holds.

The contract manager will be responsible for liaison with the provider on administration, upkeep and maintenance of assets.

5.9 IT budget management

In the past, IT budgets have often been held and managed centrally by the IT Directorate. As service contracts are introduced, budgets for IT services may continue to be centralised, or each user of services may have its own budget.

Delegating IT budgets that have previously been centralised can lead to a major change in organisational culture. An important benefit can be that business managers will have an incentive to monitor their IT services, to ensure that they are obtaining value for money, and to use IT for improving business performance. But for them to develop their experience and skills in managing budgets, devolution should be phased in.

Delegation does not mean that business managers will necessarily have complete discretion in spending IT budgets – particularly if the contract covers the delivery and management of shared infrastructure or common services. Some service contracts will involve a minimum charge to the customer. This is usually to limit the risk to the service provider of declining workloads when there are fixed costs related to the service being delivered. This can create difficulties in attributing costs to particular business units, since the costs to the customer may not be directly linked to usage.

There will often be a need for a central IT budget to pay for infrastructure and corporate services. Certain constraints may be imposed on business units by the centre when budgets are devolved, for example the use of certain standards. But this may well increase the costs for business units with limited IT budgets – the centre may choose to 'top up' their budgets to cover such costs. Alternatively the centre may use its power over IT budget allocation to enforce the use of standards at a local level.

Where IT budgets have been delegated, there will be a need for careful management to ensure that improved value for money for one business unit is not achieved at the expense of others or of the organisation as a whole.

Some conflict between corporate and business unit interests and priorities can arise. This should be anticipated with mechanisms, raising awareness of the role of standards for example, put in place to reduce or resolve conflicts.

The contract administration function (there may be one in each business unit in a federal structure) will be responsible for ensuring that the budget committed to the delivery of services under the contract is not exceeded. The contract administrator may have direct responsibility for the budget, or may have to monitor the service budgets of the various users of the service. The contract administrator will also participate in forward planning for the service and the allocation of budgets, and in defining forward commitments for future use of the service.

Seeking improvements

6

Management of service delivery, relationship management and contract administration, if done well, should between them ensure that the service delivers the required levels of quality , and that customer and provider build a constructive, open relationship. But these disciplines can only ensure that things remain as they were when the contract was signed. The customer will almost certainly wish to seek improvements in the service over time.

Ideally, the requirement for improvement should be embodied in the terms of the contract. This can be at a number of levels, from simple price or turnaround time improvements to encouraging innovation in the way services are delivered. The formal terms of the contract will of course also limit how much improvement can be requested, but it is normally possible to seek improvement within the contract terms or make alterations that will allow for improvements to be made.

Improvements that give better value for the customer organisation are a benefit in themselves, but another dimension of improvement is proactive service management and anticipating needs. This means considering how the need for the service is evolving: what future demands might be, how capacity and workload are changing. Anticipating future needs and seeking improvements will gradually move the service arrangement to a position where it can fulfil them.

The provider should be involved in these considerations, and a good working relationship will be a huge help in making improvement a reality. As always, it should be remembered that the provider must benefit too. Seeking improvements is not about extracting more from the provider against their will, but about working together to improve quality, performance, value for money, or other aspects in such a way that benefits both parties.

The provider will almost certainly be seeking improvements internally. If prices are fixed, they can increase their profit by improving efficiency; if profits are shared, they are motivated to improve economy. But the terms of the contract may not necessarily encourage them to seek improvements in areas that benefit the customer. Part of the improvement process should be to aim for alignment of objectives, so that customer and provider are working towards the same things, and both deriving benefits when they are realised.

How improvement is sought depends on the type of arrangement. It may be that a requirement for improvement is built into the contract from the beginning.

In partnership arrangements, improvements will more likely be approached by customer and provider together taking a wider view of how things are going and what could usefully be changed.

The rest of this chapter discusses some options for ways of seeking improvements.

6.1 Incentives

Incentives to improve are normally built into the contract terms. The aim of incentives is to motivate the provider to improve by offering increased profit, or some other desirable benefit, as a reward for improved performance or added value.

It is important that incentives are balanced, appropriate, and not perverse. They must encourage provider behaviour that is right for the arrangement. They should not emphasise one aspect of performance at the expense of other, perhaps less visible, aspects. The aim is value for money at all levels, rather than simple cost savings. One example of a perverse incentive would be rewarding the speed in answering letters without any measure of the quality of the responses.

For partnership arrangements, the requirement will be on building a relationship and perhaps finding new ways of fulfilling business needs, and any incentives offered should encourage these behaviours rather than creating an adversarial, cost-focused arrangement.

Some examples of incentives are:

- guaranteed or fixed levels of capacity, allowing the planning of investments and improvements by the provider
- revenue sharing, profit sharing or tariff reduction
- commercial opportunities in related areas (carefully regulated by the customer)
- opportunity for innovation: the deal gives the provider the chance to implement or devise new solutions that will improve their standing
- use of spare infrastructure capacity
- exploitation of assets, systems, data or brand.

Financial incentives should offer rewards to both parties that fairly reflect any investment they have to make to achieve the saving in the first place.

Target incentive mechanisms are often used where work is task based. The provider is given the incentive to submit optimal resource estimates for a task. This provides for the sharing, in predefined ratios, of the risks and benefits of the provider exceeding or undercutting those original estimates.

| 6.2 | Continuous improvement |

Public sector managers are under constant pressure to improve. In service management, this translates into a need for continuous improvement in the performance or value for money of providers' services. Continuous improvement should be part of improvement for the business unit as a whole, improving the performance of the contract management team as well as the service covered by the contract itself.

It is important that continuous improvement is seen as being desirable and beneficial for both parties, rather than as a means to drive down prices.

Requirements for improvements in service are often built into an outsourcing contract, the rationale being that a provider should be able to achieve economies of scale that the customer alone cannot. Indeed, achieving improvements may be one of the main motives that the organisation has for outsourcing a service. One way to embody this principle contractually is through a capped price for the service that decreases year on year, obliging the provider to improve efficiency to preserve their profit margin. However, it is important that the contract is framed carefully, in such a way that it does not impede or discourage change. Incentives such as profit sharing may help to encourage improvement where it is possible rather than enforce it at the risk of compromising quality.

There will also be the opportunity from time to time to exploit 'break-out' improvements – perhaps radical changes in the service, or the way in which it is delivered, based on technology innovation. Again, the provider needs to be motivated to pursue such opportunities – possibly by being in a position to share the benefits (and the risks).

It may be appropriate to identify a target for the level of performance improvement sought over, say, the next year, and to develop a plan in conjunction with the provider that will achieve or exceed that level of improvement. Suggestions for improvements could come from the users of the service – for example, from information provided by the service desk, from the service provider, or from the contract manager. Some contracts employ bonus schemes to direct the provider's efforts towards the customer's priorities for service improvements.

Improvements could be expressed in terms of developments such as:

- improved customer satisfaction, as measured, for example, by independent surveys

- more efficient ways of providing the specified service

- useful additions to the service

- eliminating aspects of the service that are no longer required

- use of new technologies that would provide a cheaper and/or more effective service

- changes in procedures or working practices (in customer or provider organisation)

- changes in the interface between the customer and provider organisations.

Targets for continuous improvement must be realistic. Techniques such as Balanced Scorecard, Business Excellence Model, ongoing stakeholder analysis, benchmarking (see section 3.5), and the Goal/Question/Metric approach may be helpful in determining targets.

The companion guide *How to manage Performance* has more detail on setting performance measures and useful techniques for seeking improvements.

Continuous Improvement Plans (CIPs)

It may be useful to create a written Continuous Improvement Plan (CIP) for either or both sides in the agreement. In order to succeed, CIPs need to be developed in an environment of mutual trust. The natural way to generate a CIP is as a by-product of a good working relationship between the respective contract managers, developed over time, through regular dialogue, meetings and the sharing of ideas and aims.

Any CIP should always bear in mind the intentions of the parties at the time the original contract was entered into. For example, if the plan threatens to take the provider into 'uncharted waters', way outside the scope of what was originally envisaged, the plans may not be viewed positively. Success is more likely if a bold, well-timed and innovative move captures the imagination of both parties.

6.3 Benefits based payments

If the organisation is moving through a major business change, the main priority will be achieving the benefits from implementing particular change programmes. If providers are helping the customer to achieve business change, their incentives should be linked as far as possible to the customer's objectives, so that they have an interest in the customer's success. This can be achieved by making payments to providers dependent on the realisation of benefits to the customer organisation.

This approach has the advantage of giving the provider incentives to deliver and also of ensuring that individual investments are well planned, achievable and will deliver value. Because they are conducted as discrete exercises, the concerns about guaranteeing value for money over time are largely overcome. Instead of hazarding guesses about the future at the outset of a deal, there is a clear business justification with robust benefits identified on each occasion.

A typical process involves the following steps:

- provider or customer proposes change project or investment

- customer approves project on basis of agreed cost/benefit model

- provider develops and implements IT service to support new business process (at their own risk)

- business processes are changed (customer or joint responsibility)

- parties measure resultant cost savings to customer using agreed cost/benefit model

- provider's service charges calculated as an agreed percentage of realised cost savings to customer.

A comparable technique is business benefits based contracting. When calculating the distribution of cost savings and any charges to be levied, this approach takes into account for each programme both parties' investment, direct costs, overheads, risks borne and benefits share or planned return.

For all these processes, the emphasis is on collaboration in terms of opportunity spotting and programme implementation; and on agreement in terms of construction of the investment case and articulation of both parties' risks and rewards. It is also likely that there will need to be joint involvement in the ongoing benefits realisation process, including Post Implementation Reviews. Most such arrangements are likely to be underpinned by a joint 'open books' process.

6.4 Added value

Adding value means bringing something to the arrangement that is genuinely beyond the customer organisation's capability or capacity; something that it could not source internally, even if it wished to. Service provision arrangements that add value can be highly beneficial to the organisation.

Added value can occur at three levels:

- **business benefit:** identifying new opportunities for ways to benefit the customer's business

- **capacity/capability:** infusing new skills, methodologies and capabilities in the service delivery

- **economy:** better, more efficient and cheaper services through economy of scale or rationalisation.

A provider's contribution to all three should be readily capable of identification throughout the deal either at the outset, on an ongoing basis or for individual programmes. This might also form a useful measure with which to assess their performance.

Any incentives put in place for the provider should encourage them to add value where they can.

Managing changes

7

The only constant is change. It's a cliché, but it goes to the heart of the problems that can beset large-scale service provision. A successful arrangement requires a mutual commitment to meeting evolving business requirements. What's more, properly managed change can be a good opportunity to alter or improve the service.

There will inevitably be changes to the service during the lifetime of the contract. The customer may need to vary the service, perhaps because of changes in the business. Or the provider may request changes – for example, to implement a technological improvement.

In several of the cases discussed below, the need is mentioned for provision in the contract negotiation stage, or for a thorough risk assessment before signing the contract. The companion guide *How to manage Service Acquisition* provides more detail on these earlier stages. OGC's guidance on risk may also be helpful.

The companion guide *How to manage Business Change* and the complementary guide *Managing Successful Programmes* provide more detail on the issues around change in general.

7.1 Drivers for change

The drivers for change during the term of a contract can come from a range of sources.

Internal drivers for change could include:

- evolving business requirements

- the organisational restructuring of either party

- significant revisions to the corporate strategy/business objectives of either party.

External drivers could include:

- developments in technology (things which were not possible become possible, and therefore desired or necessary to maintain the 'market' efficiency of service provision)

- economic trends that affect the profitability/value for money of the relationship – from the perspective of the customer or the provider

- the need to provide electronic forms of service delivery to meet customer expectation.

7.2 The implications of change

The importance of understanding the implications of change from the perspective of both parties cannot be overemphasised. Change to a contract affects the scope and thus the viability of the deal, for either or both parties. To an extent both parties are taking a calculated risk when they enter long-term contract arrangements that the cumulative effect of change over the term will balance out for both. It may not necessarily be so, especially over relatively short periods, and both parties need to remain conscious of the impact on themselves and on their partners.

It is essential that both parties have realistic expectations of what the deal will deliver at the outset: that the deal is neither intentionally nor inadvertently 'over-sold' by either party. This 'foundation of realism' is essential if the expectations generated by both the customer's and the provider's business cases are to be met. This is not as straightforward as it may seem, as there is often a tendency within both customer and provider organisations during the procurement phase to 'over-sell' the prospects for the deal in order to gain the necessary management approvals to proceed. This temptation must be resisted if the viability of the deal is to be maintained for both parties.

Care must also be taken not to distort the original competition, particularly the original value for money equation, as this could conflict with EC rules.

If changes reduce the scope

If the cumulative effect of change is to reduce the scope of the deal, clearly the customer will be concerned about the overall profitability of the relationship from its perspective (since, all else being equal, economies of scale will be reduced). In legal terms the customer must ensure that it is not open to claims from the provider for misrepresentation about the volume of business likely to result from the award of a particular contract or of 'false prospectus' – that is, encouraging an expectation which is not fulfilled. In any cases of doubt specialist legal advice must be sought.

If changes increase the scope

If, on the other hand, the cumulative effect of change is such as to significantly increase the scale or the scope of the services provided, the customer must have a concern that it continues to achieve value for money from the relationship overall. It must also ensure (assuming the contract to be subject to public procurement law) that the developments do not take the resulting contract:

* outside the scope of the original OJEC advertisement

* outside the permitted extensions to existing contracts allowed under the relevant regulations.

Again, in any cases of doubt specialist legal advice must be sought.

7.3 Preparing for change

Changes are always easier to manage when they are planned. Even where they occur without warning, it is often possible to foresee what might happen and plan for what can be done. This is particularly true of contingency changes.

Change to external factors may make change hard to avoid; however, alteration of the service and/or its underlying infrastructure is always voluntary. It may not always be most effective to make incremental changes to a service that is running smoothly – it may be better to accumulate such change requirements for a while and then make them *en bloc*. According to the type of provider relationships involved, the provider(s) may be closely involved in planning the changes, or may even be entirely accountable for them.

7.4 Types of change

The following sections examine four types of change that pose particular challenges for service management:

- changes to performance metrics
- changes to service functionality
- changes to service infrastructure
- changes to workload.

Changes will always need to be negotiated with the provider(s). Where there are several providers involved, special care may be needed over the knock-on effects of changes.

Changes should not be scheduled during critical business periods, such as year-end or cyclic workload peaks.

Changes to performance metrics

Changes to performance metrics may be required for several reasons:

- business service requirements may alter – for example, an electronic messaging and intranet service may become more critical to an organisation once the users have ceased to rely on paper backups
- the metrics may be found in practice to be inappropriate. For example, a messaging service may be based on an existing telecommunicationss contract which defines availability at the electronic circuit level. The end-to-end messaging service may become unreliable, even when the underlying circuits are meeting contract specification for availability
- the metrics may be difficult to measure reliably. Alternative approximations may need to be identified
- the provider may be unhappy with the metrics and may press for changes that may not be to the customer's advantage
- changes to the service infrastructure may enable better metrics to be used.

Particular care is needed when changing performance metrics, as exception reports may indicate service failures, leading to claims for service credits and so on, when, in fact, the changes are proceeding as planned. The new metrics may depend upon a period of accumulated service history, and it may be that the service is, in effect, running for a period with no effective metrics. This requires a basis of trust between customer and provider.

Changes to service functionality

Changes to service functionality may be required for several reasons, including:

- changes to the organisation's marketplace

- changes to the organisation's product/service strategy

- internal business structural or process change

- proactive suggestions by the service provider(s)

- imposed policy or legislative change.

In all cases, it is likely that there will be consequent changes to the service processes and metrics, leading to a contract variation that will need to be negotiated with the provider(s). Key principles of this renegotiation are that:

- the contract(s) should have been negotiated to provide for such change

- when seeking changes to the service supplied, these should be specified in outcome-based terms, so as to allow the provider to propose innovative solutions where appropriate

- changes to service function will almost always lead to changes to the performance metrics

- sometimes there may arise a threshold where a series of incremental changes leads to an accumulation of short-term expedients that together are unsatisfactory. At this point, a more drastic overhaul of the service infrastructure may become a better proposition

- the customer should always beware of the possibility of the provider seeking to increase their profitability – solutions and the associated costs proposed by the provider should always be rigorously audited for best value.

As with changes to performance metrics, there may be anomalies in service management and reporting during periods of functional change.

Major change to service functionality may require the re-activation of a programme management mode of operation for a period.

Changes to service infrastructure

Changes may be required to:

- business process
- technical infrastructure.

Selection and timing of such changes may be wholly or partially at the discretion of the provider(s). If the customer requires the provider to make changes to the service infrastructure, they should remember that, by limiting the provider's discretion, they may be, in effect, relieving the provider of some of their contractual obligations, to the point where the provider may be able to disclaim responsibility for a subsequent service failure.

Major change to service infrastructure may require the re-activation of a programme management mode of operation for a period.

Changes to workload

Business workloads may increase to the point where the customer believes that the provider is gaining increased economies of scale – leading to an opportunity to renegotiate unit costs. However, there may be a different perception from the provider; they may have the view that the unforeseen increase in workload is leading to the need to replace capital items early, leading to an increase in unit costs. Such negotiations are always much easier if the provision for such changes has been embodied in the underlying contract(s).

The ability of a service provision relationship to accommodate change effectively and efficiently is fundamental to its success. This is particularly true for IT services, which must be capable of accommodating fundamental change to all key aspects if they are not to risk frustrating the organisation's ability to develop its business and enhance efficiency. IT services must promise business advantage to the client over the term of the contract, together with access to the latest technology. If they do not, or when they fail to deliver it, strategic objectives are unlikely to be fulfilled.

7.5 The IT perspective

In long-term IT service agreements, the customer may be looking to a provider for:

- access to IT related skills and expertise which the customer cannot provide in-house (or by other means)
- an IT service that will act as an enabler of change and improvement in existing business processes and/or business efficiency
- a source of fresh ideas and innovation to benefit the business.

A key part of the rationale for entering the deal, from the customer perspective, is to ensure that the latest developments in technology are available to meet emerging business requirements over time and that, in business terms, the organisation remains 'competitive' in whatever business environment it operates.

IT infrastructure management

8

IT infrastructure management refers to the IT business processes that control the quality, efficiency and effectiveness of IT services. It brings together people, processes, organisation and technologies to support the objectives of its customers' business.

It may well be that the organisation no longer takes on the responsibility for managing its own infrastructure, and that this has been passed on to a provider organisation. The guidance in this chapter assumes that this is the case; in other words, it deals with the service provision issues that pertain particularly to IT infrastructure management being carried out on the organisation's behalf by a provider.

8.1 Why is infrastructure management important?

In order to deliver business at agreed service levels in today's fast-changing business environments, ongoing infrastructure management is needed. Successful delivery of IT services and business continuity plans will often depend on supporting IT infrastructure. Improvements to IT infrastructure may form the basis for gains in efficiency, new methods of service delivery and other business benefits.

Despite this, it is notoriously difficult to justify infrastructure projects in a business case. The benefits of improving infrastructure may be long term, indirect, or enabling benefits (those that enable other, strategic benefits to be realised). But the costs may still be high.

The purpose of infrastructure management is to model the mixture of technical components (hardware, software and communications facilities), their geographical distribution, and how they support or implement the business systems and other parts of the information system architecture environment within the department.

The public sector perspective

It is now recognised that rapid increase in electronic interchange of data can dramatically simplify and improve the majority of public sector and business processes, in particular the effective interoperation between the physical infrastructures of all parties.

For the public sector, a key challenge in the implementation of Information Age Government is that existing IT infrastructures have largely been established based on departmental or agency boundaries. Each is subject to one or more existing external contracts, some are PFI based and long term, and in some the provider is responsible for IT strategy, and even for business process change.

The business perspective	It is essential that the business understands the implications of infrastructure decisions. Although the IT infrastructure is in many respects a concern of the IT provider, it is also of importance to the customer organisation's business, if it is to avoid 'lock-in' to a particular technical approach. The business may wish to use a new technology in an innovative way to support or bring about a new way of doing business. Infrastructure needs to be managed across corporate and business area levels. The infrastructure may have to support several business areas, of varying degrees of autonomy, to facilitate the co-ordination of their activities, for example, through information sharing. Irrespective of who owns the infrastructure, the business information that it makes available has to be in the right place at the right time.
8.2 Who is involved?	Strategic planners first define the nature of the infrastructure required, as part of IT strategy definition. It is then the responsibility of business management to manage providers' definition and delivery of infrastructure; providers are responsible for the everyday management of infrastructure.
	The customer organisation may wish to retain control over the technical policy for the IT infrastructure and ownership of its business and IT architectural design.
8.3 Defining the IT infrastructure	To establish what infrastructure and levels of support are needed, consider the following questions:

- what infrastructure is already in place?

- where is it?

- how well is it working?

- how much is it costing?

- how well is it supporting the organisation's business/IT strategy?

The infrastructure provides the support and linkages for the other architectural components; it cannot be fully developed until the other architectural components have been defined and developed in some detail. It describes the available technology and the limitation of technology on business requirements, business patterns and business methods. It focuses on the performance of the information systems in support of the organisation and addresses standards and security issues.

To define the infrastructure, special consideration needs to be given to concepts being defined in the other architectural components, such as the work locations and user groups in the work architecture. However, by adhering to infrastructure principles and standards, one can scope the infrastructure components using commercial off-the-shelf (COTS) software, compatible hardware and common hardware.

8.4 The provider's responsibilities

The provider is responsible for these day-to-day management processes:

- capacity management: ensuring that the infrastructure can support the volumes of demand required and can cope with peaks and troughs in demand

- availability: ensuring that network services are available within the time periods agreed in the contract (during normal office hours, for example)

- cost: keeping costs to agreed parameters for service delivery

- service levels: maintaining agreed levels in terms of volume and service quality

- configuration: providing and updating changes to services as required

- service continuity: ensuring that the business has access to the required services and providing contingency arrangements in the event of disaster such as floods

- relationship management: providing the interface between provider and customer (and with third party providers as required).

8.5 Interoperability

Most recently, developments in thinking on IT infrastructure have opened the way to far greater integration and cheap, flexible connectivity between the systems and networks of diverse organisations. Corporate computing resources should be interconnected to promote interoperability consistent with information technology policy. Infrastructure development should adhere to defined standards, including those for interoperability.

For more information on interoperability standards, see the government interoperability framework (e-GIF) documentation.

8.6 Managing infrastructure risk

Risks that the customer should be aware of include:

- business/contractual relationship failure

- need for the service(s) fails to mature or reach critical mass

- failure to deliver the required business outcome because the infrastructure is unfit in terms of functionality, flexibility, throughput and/or security

- failure to sustain service or achieve value for money because technology is bypassed by better/cheaper options to which economic migration is not possible

- technological blind alley – failure to evolve

- loss of in-house capability to manage the service effectively and/or to recompete it

- failure to interoperate (note that compliance with the e-government interoperability framework is mandatory for central government).

**8.7 Key factors
for success**

An IT infrastructure must:

- have a clearly defined business rationale

- support the sharing of information between users and across business applications

- be able to move application systems between different hardware and software platforms

- ensure the underlying technology is invisible to the user

- adhere to defined standards, including those for interoperability (Open Systems Integration)

- adhere to well articulated management and technical policies

- have clear management ownership and responsibility for infrastructure components

- ensure the demands on staff resources are realistic

- take advantage of economies of scale

- be compatible between infrastructure components, making change possible without disruption

- have clear, well-designed change management processes and procedures.

Recompetition

9

Recompetition is what happens at the end of a contract – the exit strategy from the old contract and the process of creating a new one. The larger the contract, the more attention needs to be paid to recompetition.

This chapter explores the options at the end of a contract. It seeks to provide a framework for the decision-making processes surrounding recompetition and to highlight the issues to be addressed in ensuring a successful handover.

9.1 The benefits of recompetition

For the customer, the process of recompetition can be desirable because:

- it provides an opportunity to gain leverage, extracting better value and service than might otherwise have been obtained

- it provides an incentive for providers to become more innovative in their solutions to the challenges faced by the customer. New offerings in the market can be given a chance to compete, and the incumbent will need to produce more imaginative solutions to the challenges faced to stand a chance of winning

- it allows for greater flexibility, necessary to comply with the customer organisation's strategic needs. The contract can be re-scoped to accommodate changes in the business plan

- it forces the customer to re-evaluate needs, subject to the rigorous preparation of a new business case. Without recompetition and with many other pressures on management time, there may otherwise be a temptation simply to extend the contract on similar terms, on the basis that it has worked well so far. Preparing the business case for the recompetition may result in a fresh appraisal of needs, leading to a solution more in accordance with the business strategy.

A carefully considered exit strategy is also important in helping to reduce the potentially overwhelming advantage of the incumbent provider. There should be a clearly prepared exit strategy from the outset of the relationship, not just at recompetition. It should be seen as a confidence builder, providing a reassuring safety net for both parties, not as 'planning for disaster'.

Recompetition is both necessary and desirable. Organisations must face up to it early and not underestimate the challenges involved in both successfully planning and implementing the search for the new provider and managing the handover.

9.2 Reassessing business need

Recompetition starts with a return to the business need that gave rise to the acquisition of the service in the first place. Other issues, such as what kind of arrangement is appropriate for the new procurement, and the scope of the new contract, should 'cascade' from business need.

The first step is to establish what, if any, needs there actually will be for the foreseeable future. The high-level drivers need to be considered, so that the nature of the business needs both now and in the future can be evaluated.

This means considering questions such as:

- does the old contract still meet business need?
- if a new arrangement on similar lines is created, will it meet needs in the future as well as now?
- which of the services delivered under the old contract are still required?
- are there new requirements?
- how could the new requirements be met?
- what initiatives (government-wide and departmental) will impact on this recompetition?
- what kind of arrangement is appropriate now?
- has sufficient expertise been retained to be sure of running a successful re-procurement?

Figure 4 (opposite) outlines the process of recompetition. The steps followed and the questions asked will mirror the original procurement in many ways, but will now take account of developments in business needs, policy demands, market developments and the lessons learned from the contract.

Other organisations

Other public sector organisations should also be considered:

- what business requirements does the organisation have in common with others in the public sector that can be jointly sourced, or which can be provided through another's sourcing arrangements?
- has another organisation set up a framework agreement for commodity services that could be used?
- do the terms of the existing framework allow for the addition of new customers?

Figure 4
Planning the recompetition

A flowchart showing the questions that should be asked and the options at each stage. Note the identification of needs that precedes any consideration of the contract arrangements, influenced by outside factors such as policy, strategy and government initiatives

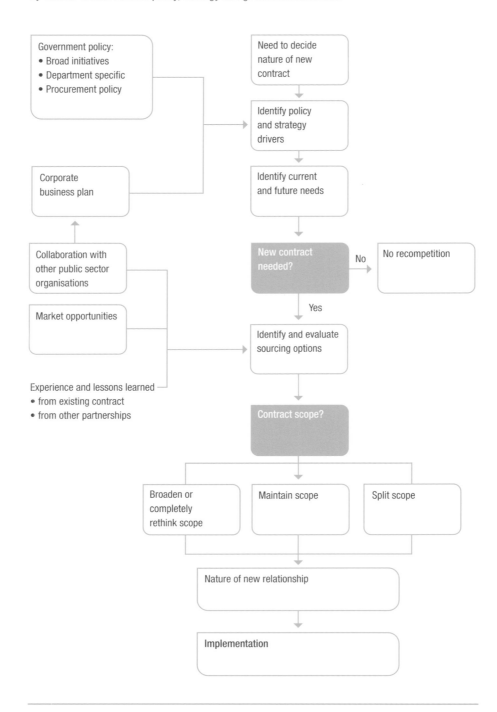

Look at the experiences of others in the public sector to identify opportunities for improvement. There needs to be a greater appreciation of the importance of a well-planned exit strategy, which reduces the hold of the incumbent and smoothes the transition. This includes providing financial incentives for the provider to perform well right up to the end of the contract.

9.3 Looking at sourcing options

As with the initial acquisition, once business need has been identified, the options for sourcing need to be examined. The issues to consider are:

- how best to provide currently outsourced services for which there will be a future need

- how best to provide services currently supplied in-house, for which there will be a future need

- how best to provide services for which there will be only a limited future need

- how best to provide totally new services or capture new means of providing existing services.

Consider first the existing relationship. In deciding what form a future outsourcing might take, there is clearly much to learn from the current relationship. What scope is there for improvement? This can take the form of a systematic evaluation of different aspects of the relationship, either internally or with the advice of external consultancy.

Factors to consider include:

- range of services

- flexibility of contract

- customer's reaction and adjustment to outsourcing

- exit strategy

- 'informed partner' capabilities

- quality and focus of service: did the provider deliver services to a high quality and on time? Were the provider's incentives structured to ensure buy-in to the customer's objectives?

Scoping scenarios

The key decision to be addressed is the scope of the new contract or contracts. The options are:

- to retain the scope of the existing contract

- to split the scope of the existing contract

- to broaden the scope of the existing contract, perhaps to expand it into a strategic alliance or partnership

- to completely rethink the requirement for the contract.

Cascading from this scoping decision will be the nature of the new contract or contracts; what kind of relationship is required with a provider, including its length and funding arrangements?

Note that bringing services back in-house once they have been contracted out is not listed as an option. This is an extreme measure, often not viable (particularly if the decision to outsource was properly thought through); the skills will not be available in-house to make it possible.

The decision will, of course, be dependent upon the individual circumstances of the organisation. However, many organisations will face similar issues. The first thing to do is to look at the key options that involve changing the scope. These are summarised in table 1.

Table 1
Options for broadening or splitting the scope of a procurement

Broaden scope	Split scope
Combine services under single provider	Split services to multiple providers
Add value added services, such as Business Process Re-engineering	
Add high-risk tailored services	Separate out services for commodity provision
Perhaps through joint procurement	*Perhaps through joint procurement*

Broadening the scope may be a matter of taking functions currently managed by different providers and bundling them into one package. Conversely, the recompetition may be used as an opportunity to widen the range of providers or split services off for commodity provision.

One provider or more?

The decision on single or multiple providers is not straightforward; the number of providers must be decided on a case-by-case basis. A possible compromise is the lead provider approach, where one provider is given overall responsibility for managing sub-providers. This does not give the customer the same level of control over the sub-providers and can lengthen the supply chain, but otherwise captures many advantages of both solutions.

If there are already several interdependent contracts making up the service, the issues to be considered will include:

* what is the effect on the overall service of replacing one component of it?

* should the entire service be reconstituted on a different basis?

* if so, how should the ends of the component contracts be synchronised?

What kind of contract?   There is a broad trend towards relationships becoming more sophisticated, extending towards higher value added processes such as control of business functions. This represents a major re-evaluation of the relationship between customers and providers. Concurrent with this change in scope must be a development in the nature of the relationship: a deepening of the partnership.

If it is decided that a new contract along similar lines to the old one is in the best interests of the organisation, then special care must be taken in managing the recompetition. How will an open and fair recompetition be ensured? How will other potential providers be encouraged to bid? In the absence of substantial competition, how will the best possible value for money deal be obtained? If there is a change in provider, then all the implementation challenges associated with other recompetitions still apply.

9.4   The handover   Careful planning and management of the handover from incumbent to new provider(s) is of crucial importance to ensuring business continuity.

The handover process is driven by the need to ensure business continuity during a period of major upheaval. This is especially important if the handover is mid-project. In addition, public sector organisations have an obligation in law, and as a matter of public policy, to do what they can to create the environment for an effective and open competitive environment (the 'level playing field'). Whether this is an easy task or not will depend on a number of factors.

The key issues that need to be addressed when a commercial agreement is approaching its conclusion are:

* investment towards the end of the relationship

* people issues

* the end-to-end lead time that will be required to get a new provider up and running

* handover obligations on the potentially outgoing provider

* physical assets (that is, IT equipment and other tangible property)

* software

* data.

In considering the handover, special attention should be given to the assurance of business continuity and how to ensure a genuine competition in the presence of a potential advantage to the incumbent. Begin planning the exit strategy early, at the procurement stage, and include a transfer of responsibility agreement. Consider incentives for a successful handover, such as retention of funds or asset inspection – see HM Treasury guidance on Standardisation of PFI Contracts (IT) for more detailed advice.

Finally, there are occasional circumstances where a delay to the recompetition is desirable on business grounds. Properly handled, this could be in the long-term interests of effective competition.

This chapter explores in more depth the functional roles and responsibilities involved in service provision.

The important roles (functions) are:

- business unit manager – responsible for the area of the business that depends on successful service delivery for the achievement of its business objectives

- service manager – who, following service inception, assumes responsibility for oversight of the effectiveness of the service. This is a key intelligent customer function (see section 2.1).

- contract manager (on both customer and provider sides) – responsible for the formal governance of the contract. If the service is made up of a number of agreements or contracts, each such contract will have a contract manager on both the customer and the provider side

- relationship manager – takes responsibility for ongoing communications, common understanding and shared information between all the parties involved

- component managers – take reponsibility for individual components of the service, if it is extensive enough to be divided up in this way

- customer support personnel (for each component if applicable)

- the customer – the end recipient of the service, who may be a corporate entity or a private citizen. The customer could be the business unit for delivery of internal IT and/or business services.

It is possible, particularly for smaller contracts, that the service manager, contract manager and relationship manager roles may be filled by the same group or individual (with the obvious exception of the provider's contract manager).

Experience has shown that it is vital to define consistent levels of communication between equivalent contacts in customer and provider – that is, pairs of people at each level in the respective organisations who discuss issues relevant to their level of authority. (See section 4.2 for more detail on communication levels.)

Where contract management expertise is not available in-house, it may be appropriate to buy in advice from professional consultants, or even appoint a professional contract manager. Such arrangements must be clearly defined to ensure that ownership of the arrangement remains with the customer; it is also important to safeguard commercial confidence when third parties are involved.

10.1 Business manager The main functional responsibilities of the business manager are to:

- identify business requirement and ensure that the statement of business requirements (SBR) or statement of service requirements (SSR) is prepared and maintained

- set/maintain/develop the service strategy

- arrange for the constitution of a programme or service board as necessary; chair this board

- review and approve relevant aspects of IT and infrastructure strategy

- oversee interpretation of business requirement into the service specification

- monitor performance at the level of business outcome

- oversee evolution of the service in response to changing business needs.

10.2 Service manager The main functional responsibilities of the service manager are to:

- following service inception, assume responsibility from the programme manager for oversight of the effectiveness of the service

- track interpretation of business requirement into the service specification

- establish service performance metrics and maintain specification of them

- monitor service performance and report it at business outcome level

- set and monitor subordinate performance metrics

- manage escalated exceptions

- escalate major exceptions as appropriate

- involve and support the service board as necessary

- represent the customer's interests to the provider at the overall level

- according to contractual placement of accountability, operate relevant aspects of the top-level service according to the service specification

- oversee development of the infrastructure strategy according to the contractually allocated responsibilities

- oversee development of the supporting infrastructure according to the contractually allocated responsibilities.

10.3 Contract manager/contract management team The size of the contract team will vary according to the nature of the arrangement and may also change over the life of the contract. The team must be given enough time, and have enough experience, to handle the contractual arrangements properly.

On large contracts, customers typically need to allow for resources equal to around 2% of the contract's value to be devoted to managing it. For smaller contracts, the percentage rises. More resources will also be required during the difficult stage of implementation.

Customer side

The main functional responsibilities of the contract manager on the customer side are to:

- track the interpretation of business requirement into contractual provisions
- maintain the specification of contract performance metrics
- monitor contract performance and report at overall service or business outcome level
- monitor subordinate performance metrics as appropriate
- represent the customer's interests to the provider at contract level
- oversee operation of the contract(s)
- determine and take remedial actions by agreement with the provider
- negotiate remedies with the provider
- escalate contract problems as necessary
- maintain/develop contract specifications.

Provider side

The main functional responsibilities of the contract manager on the provider side are to:

- track the interpretation of the business requirement into contractual provisions
- monitor contract performance and report at service/business outcome level as appropriate
- monitor subordinate performance metrics
- identify and manage exceptions
- represent the provider's interests to the customer
- respond to changing customer needs
- marshal and apply the provider's resources
- determine and take remedial actions by agreement with the customer
- negotiate remedies with the customer
- escalate problems as necessary

- operate the contract to specification

- operate subordinate services/contracts

- maintain/develop service components

- set/maintain/develop infrastructure strategy according to the contractually allocated responsibilities

- maintain/develop supporting infrastructure according to the contractually allocated responsibilities.

10.4 Relationship managers

The main functional responsibilities of the relationship managers on the customer and provider side are to:

- encourage an atmosphere of trust, openness and communication and an attitude based on working together and shared objectives

- proactively look for ways to improve the relationship wherever possible

- ensure that all stakeholders in the arrangement feel that they are involved, that their views are important and that they are acted upon

- establish and manage a communication framework and ensure that it is used effectively

- establish and manage communication flows between customer and provider, and ensure that they are used

- ensure that communications at all levels are peer-to-peer

- manage the dispute resolution process

- resolve 'soft' tensions between customer and provider, that is, situations where tension is felt or perceived but no formal issue has yet arisen

- 'manage upwards' to ensure that senior management are informed about issues before they escalate, and can intervene as appropriate

- establish regular reporting procedures, both formal and informal, and ensure that they are used

- organise forums, working groups, seminars, roadshows, training sessions and other information-sharing activities involving staff from both the customer and the provider side

- promote understanding of each other's business practices and common techniques

It is vital that the relationship managers have the authority to make or suggest changes to the arrangement – working practices, communication flows, the contract itself – to ensure that the relationship is safeguarded.

10.5 Customer support   The main functional responsibilities of the customer support manager are to:

- provide a customer support service according to the contract
- provide a first line advice and support service
- pursue incidents and problems to resolution
- monitor performance of the customer support service according to metrics as agreed
- represent customer needs and issues to service and component managers for consideration of response/remedy
- escalate problems as necessary.

10.6 The user   The main functional responsibilities of the user (that is, any person or business unit that is the recipient of services) are to:

- utilise the service
- report incidents, problems and issues promptly and accurately
- monitor customer aspects of service quality
- escalate problems as necessary.

Annexes

A Relationship management checklist

B The OGC IT Infrastructure Library (ITIL)

Relationship management checklist

A

Managing the relationship is a vital part of service management. This checklist covers some key questions to ask of your arrangements for relationship management.

General

- Do you feel that the relationship works for your organisation?

- Is the relationship well regarded at all levels of the organisation? Are the views of those at other levels taken into account when assessing the relationship?

- Do you know how the service provider feels about the relationship?

- Do customer and provider regard each other positively?

- Is there an atmosphere of mutual trust and openness about the relationship?

- Do the behaviour and attitude of those involved in the relationship reflect that kind of atmosphere?

- Has the relationship responded positively and flexibly to the need for change and to any issues that have arisen?

- Is the right tone for the relationship being set by senior management?

The relationship manager

- Is there a nominated person responsible for managing the relationship?

- Does the relationship manager have Intelligent Customer skills and capabilities, that is, do they understand both parties' businesses and objectives?

- Does the relationship manager's background and experience make them suitable for managing this relationship?

- Do staff on both sides respect the knowledge and authority of the relationship manager?

- Does the relationship manager have the authority to make decisions and commit resource on the organisation's behalf? If not, do they have direct access to those who do?

Communication

- Have communication flows and peer-to-peer relationships between customer and provider been established?

- Are there regular meetings with the service provider?

- Do meetings have specific objectives that are clearly understood by both sides?

- Are issues raised early enough to be addressed quickly and effectively?

- Are people willing to try and solve problems?

- Are there any contacts with the provider that you should have, but do not?

- Do customer and provider share information effectively?

Governance

- Is there disagreement over lines of responsibility?

- Is change control being used to manage changes to the contract?

- Are formal dispute resolution and escalation procedures in place, and are they being used?

- Are charging patterns as expected?

The OGC IT Infrastructure Library (ITIL)

IT service providers are concerned with ensuring that the service they provide is effective and efficient, offering the best possible support to their customers' business. ITIL (the OGC IT Infrastructure Library) is a body of guidance aimed initially at helping IT service providers. However, the principles set out in ITIL are generic, and will be useful to any service providers. ITIL provides the practical backing on the provider side for the principles outlined in this book, with management techniques and processes to ensure flexible, reliable service provision that supports the customer organisation through business change.

ITIL is the most widely accepted approach to IT service management in the world. ITIL provides a comprehensive and consistent set of best practices for IT service management, promoting a quality approach to achieving business effectiveness and efficiency in the use of information systems.

ITIL serves as a common language enabling all within an organisation to describe and understand processes and aspects of service management.

ITIL is based on the collective experience of commercial and governmental practitioners worldwide, distilled into one reliable, coherent approach. ITIL is fast becoming a *de facto* standard used by some of the world's leading blue-chip businesses.

There are three main benefits in using providers who adopt the ITIL standard.

- **Better customer services.** ITIL enables providers to deliver better services tailored to the specific needs of their customers. By offering services which have been designed and developed in consultation with the customer, based upon effective and appropriate underlying principles, the customer's working practices, goals and objectives can be more readily matched.

- **Better cost effectiveness.** ITIL principles have been designed to facilitate providers' quality management of services, and of the infrastructure. This best practice approach is intended to assist providers to deliver a quality service within a business environment affected by budgetary constraints, skill shortages, system complexity, rapid change, current and future user requirements and growing user expectations.

- **Better motivation and productivity.** Within the provider organisation, ITIL encourages staff to view service management as a recognised professional skill, especially through the qualifications and training available. Competence sets can be readily defined and provider staff focus on the right tasks, improving provider performance.

Key components of ITIL

- **Service support** focuses on ensuring that the customer has access to appropriate services to support business functions. Tasks involved include service desk, incident management, problem management, configuration management, change management and release management.

- **Service delivery** covers all the aspects that must be considered to offer business users adequate support. Issues covered include service level management, financial management for services, service continuity management, availability management, contingency planning and capacity management. It makes explicit the links and principal relationships between all the service management processes and other infrastructure management processes.

- **Security management** covers the process of security management with service management. It focuses on the process of implementing security requirements identified in the Service Level Agreement, rather than considering business issues of security policy.

- **The business perspective** concerns the understanding and provision of services. Topics addressed include business continuity management, partnerships and outsourcing, surviving change and transformation of business practices through radical change.

- **ICT infrastructure management** covers design and planning, deployment, technical support and operations.

- **Application management** covers the entire application lifecycle and also supports business change, with emphasis on clear requirement definition and implementation of solutions.

ITIL titles covering these components are available from The Stationery Office and Format Publishing. See the further information section opposite for more details.

Further information

OGC publications

IS Management and
Business Change Guides

- *How to manage Business Change* (ISBN 1903091101)
- *How to manage Service Acquisition* (ISBN 190309111X)
- *How to manage Performance* (ISBN 1903091136)
- *How to manage Business and IT Strategies* (ISBN 1903091020)
- *Managing Partnerships* (ISBN 1903091063)
- *IS Strategy: process and products* (ISBN 1903091004)

CD-ROM versions are also available. Available from Format Publishing (www.formatpublishing.co.uk) and The Stationery Office (www.tso.co.uk).

OGC IT Infrastructure
Library (ITIL)

- *Service Support* (ISBN 0113300158)
- *Service Delivery* (ISBN 0113300174)
- *Security Management* (ISBN 011330014X
- *Planning to Implement Service Management* (ISBN 0113308779)
- *Application Management* (ISBN 0113308663)
- *Infrastructure Management* (ISBN 0113308655)
- *The Business Perspective* (ISBN 0113308949)

CD-ROM versions are also available. Available from Format Publishing (www.formatpublishing.co.uk) and The Stationery Office (www.tso.co.uk).

Programme and
Project Management

- *Managing Successful Programmes* (ISBN 0113300166)
- *Managing Successful Projects with PRINCE 2* (ISBN 0113308558)

Available from Format Publishing and The Stationery Office.

Other OGC publications

- *OGC Model Agreements* (CD-ROM ISBN 0113308957)
- *OGC P&CD's Guide to appointment of consultants*
- *Business System Development with SSADM*
- *OGC Successful Delivery Toolkit* (available online at www.ogc.gov.uk)

For more information about OGC's products and services, call the OGC Service Desk on 0845 000 4999 or visit the OGC website at www.ogc.gov.uk

HM Treasury publications

Treasury Taskforce Technical Note: Appointing and managing advisers – available on the OGC website (www.ogc.gov.uk)

Index